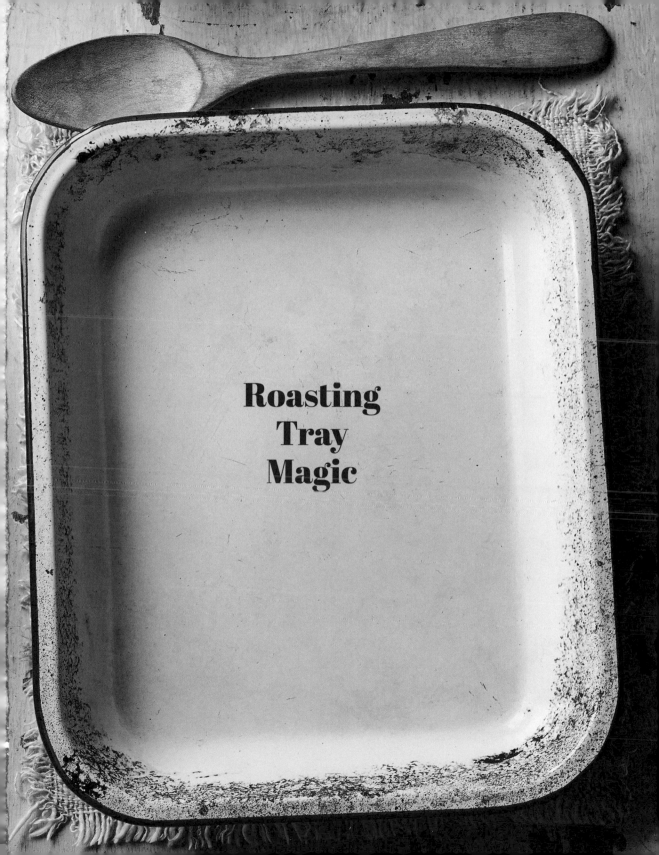

Roasting
Tray
Magic

Sue Quinn

Roasting Tray Magic

One tin, one meal, no fuss!

Photography by Faith Mason

quadrille

Publishing Director: Sarah Lavelle
Creative Director: Helen Lewis
Commissioning Editor: Céline Hughes
Designer: Gemma Hayden
Design Assistant: Shani Travers
Photography: Faith Mason
Prop Stylist: Luis Peral
Food Stylist: Rosie Reynolds
Food Stylist Assistant: Jess Dennison
Production Controller: Nikolaus Ginelli
Production Director: Vincent Smith

First published in 2017 by Quadrille,
an imprint of Hardie Grant Publishing

Quadrille
52–54 Southwark Street
London SE1 1UN
quadrille.com

Reprinted in 2017, 2018
10 9 8 7 6 5 4 3

Cataloguing in Publication Data: a catalogue record for this book
is available from the British Library.

ISBN: 978 1 78713 012 8

Printed in China

Contents

Introduction

There's no getting away from the fact that cooking often involves a little bit of drudgery. Complicated recipes to follow, multiple pots to stir and mountains of washing up can make cooking seem like hard graft, especially on weeknights when time is short and people just want to eat. There's a place for complicated dishes, of course, but even enthusiastic home cooks often want food that is simple to make, delicious to eat and doesn't entail using every pot in the kitchen. So, for those who haven't fallen under the spell of roasting tray magic before, this book might well be a revelation.

Every recipe within these pages – snacks, starters, complete meals, warm salads and desserts – requires just one roasting tray to make. Such a surprisingly wide range of dishes emphasises just how underrated this humble piece of kitchen equipment is. But roasting tray cooking does more than just smooth the culinary path when your cooking mojo is low and demand for a tasty meal is high; it also delivers food that is especially delicious.

Why don't roasting trays play a more prominent role in everyday home cooking? As it turns out, the concept is relatively new. As food historian Bee Wilson explains in her book *Consider the Fork: A History of How We Cook and Eat*, for hundreds of years chefs in European kitchens considered ovens to be suitable only for baking things like bread. Meat and game, meanwhile, were roasted over an open flame.

According to Wilson, this division continued until the early twentieth century, which goes some way to explain why stovetops have been the default method for cooking vegetables and smaller cuts of meat until relatively recently.

Restaurant chefs are now well versed in the benefits of roasting tray cooking; stick your head around the door of a professional kitchen and you're likely to see all manner of foods going into the oven in trays, from fillets of fish to vegetables. Chefs use this technique because it simplifies the cooking process and delivers wonderfully tasty results. Home cooks have been a little slower to catch on to the benefits; in domestic kitchens, roasting trays are still most strongly associated with cakes and joints of meat – food that doesn't readily cook on the stovetop. Hopefully this book will help change that.

Food roasted in the oven is not only convenient, but also especially flavoursome. During roasting, dry heat wraps itself around the food, locking in and concentrating flavours. At a high heat, roasted food turns gloriously burnished because the natural sugars caramelise on the outside, sealing in the juices on the inside.

Make friends with your roasting tray

All the recipes in this book have been developed and tested in a rectangular **roasting tray measuring 30 x 20 x 5cm**. For some of the snacky dishes, such as chicken scratchings, sausage rolls, corn fritters, whole Camembert and the like, the size of the tray isn't crucial, so long as the food isn't crowded together (in which case it will steam). For dishes where the food fills the tray to a particular height, like porridge, brownies, bread rolls and cake, it's important to use the recommended size, otherwise they might not cook successfully, and/or in the specified time. For dishes such as Chicken Thighs with Creamy Leek and Caper Sauce (on page 117) it's best to use the recommended tray size; something larger, for example, could see the sauce spread too thin and burn.

In fact, if you want to make the most of this book, it would be a good idea to invest in a roasting tray of the recommended size. It won't accommodate an enormous Christmas turkey, obviously, but how often do you use a roasting tray that large? What you will have, though, is a single piece of versatile kitchen equipment that's ideal for cooking a wide range of dishes, from cakes to joints of meat.

If you're shopping for a new roasting tray, use the same rule that applies for pans and baking sheets: opt for something solid and the best quality that you can afford. Steel/stainless steel (or multi-layered stainless steel and aluminium), anodised aluminium and cast iron are popular choices; or, if you want to break the bank, copper is wonderful. A heavier tray resists warping and distributes the heat more evenly, so your cooking results will be better overall. And make sure you're buying the right size: the measurements previously mentioned refer to the inside measurements of the tray.

Go for a roasting tray with rounded corners for easy cleaning, as well as handles for safely transferring it in and out of the oven. A couple of recipes in this book call for cooking food on a rack on top of the roasting tray as well as inside it; some trays come with racks when you buy them, which is great but not essential. An ordinary metal rack, or even the oven rack itself, can serve the purpose by simply sitting on top.

A final word on the vagaries of ovens: for a variety of reasons, all ovens have their own temperaments. Age, make, model, insulation and settings are all factors that can affect the accuracy of an oven's temperature reading, and therefore the expected time it takes a dish to cook. What's more, heat can vary across different parts of the oven chamber, so even using an oven thermometer does not completely solve the problem. Roasting tray cooking is a brilliantly convenient way to cook, but you can't just wander off; it requires you to keep an occasional eye on things, turn the tray round now and then (except when baking cakes, as the sudden drop in temperature can cause your masterpiece to sink or crack) and keep your senses alert for when the dish is done.

Happy roasting tray cooking!

Breakfast
+
Brunch

Roast pear and rhubarb compote

Tongue-tingling rhubarb and sweet fragrant pears are always a heady combination, and the Christmassy notes from the spices means there's a whole lot to love in a bowl of this compote. It also makes an easy pudding; swap the yoghurt for some lightly whipped vanilla-spiked cream, and maybe some ginger biscuits crumbled on top instead of nuts.

400g rhubarb, cut into 6-cm pieces,
    sliced lengthways if very thick
4 ripe but firm Conference or
    Bartlett pears
squeeze of lemon juice
120g caster sugar
1 cinnamon stick
2 cloves
1 star anise

To serve:
Greek yoghurt
4 tbsp chopped toasted hazelnuts

Serves: 4 | Takes: 25 minutes

Preheat the oven to 200°C/400°F.

Place the rhubarb in a 30 x 20 x 5-cm roasting tray. Peel, core and chop the pears into pieces the length and width of your index finger. Add them to the tray as you go, tossing with a little lemon juice to prevent discolouration.

Sprinkle the sugar over the fruit and add the spices to the tray. Toss to combine well, then cover tightly with foil and roast for 15 minutes. Remove the foil; the fruit should be very tender but if not, return to the oven, uncovered, for a further 5 minutes or so.

Serve the compote and the tray juices with a spoonful of yoghurt and the hazelnuts sprinkled over the top.

Dutch pancake with raisins, orange blossom and marmalade

Making one big pancake is much easier than standing at the stove endlessly flipping, and this one is gorgeously fragrant with oranges and raisins. If you are not in possession of marmalade, or if you aren't partial to it, just use a good-quality jam or fruit compote of your choice.

2 tbsp vegetable oil
130g plain flour
2 tbsp golden caster sugar
pinch of salt
3 large eggs, lightly beaten
300ml milk
2 tsp orange blossom water
1 tsp vanilla extract
finely grated zest of 1 orange
60g mixed raisins
good-quality marmalade, to serve

Serves: 4 | Takes: 35 minutes

Preheat the oven to 220°C/425°F. Pour the vegetable oil into a 30 x 20 x 5-cm roasting tray and place inside the oven to heat.

Whisk the flour, sugar and salt together in a mixing bowl. Whisk the eggs, milk, orange blossom water, vanilla and orange zest together in a jug. Gradually stir the wet ingredients into the dry, incorporating the flour as you go to make a smooth batter.

Working quickly, remove the roasting tray from the oven and pour in the batter. Sprinkle over the raisins and gently nudge them under the batter if necessary. Return to the oven and bake for 20 minutes, or until puffed, golden and just cooked through. Serve hot, spread with the marmalade.

Shakshuka

This version of the now famous North African dish is super easy as it completely cooks itself in the oven, allowing you to get on with important stuff like reading the weekend papers.

1 large red onion, halved and thickly
   sliced, layers separated
2 large red peppers, sliced
2 tbsp olive oil
200g chorizo, cut into 2-cm cubes
2 x 400-g cans chopped tomatoes
3 garlic cloves, crushed
2 tsp hot paprika
2 tsp ground cumin
1 heaped tbsp rose harissa paste
4–6 large eggs
200g feta cheese, crumbled
handful of coriander leaves and tender
   stems, roughly chopped

Serves: 4–6 | Takes: 1 hour 10 minutes

Preheat the oven to 200°C/400°F.

Place all the ingredients, except the eggs, feta and coriander, in a 30 x 20 x 5-cm roasting tray. Add 150ml water and stir well so all the ingredients are combined. Bake for 45 minutes, stirring frequently and adding a splash more water towards the end of cooking if needed to prevent the sauce becoming too thick.

Make indentations in the sauce with a spoon and crack in the eggs. Bake for about 10 minutes more, but watch the eggs carefully so the yolks don't overcook: the yolks need to be gooey. Sprinkle over the feta and coriander and serve immediately.

Cinnamon French toast

French toast is really just an excuse to eat dessert for breakfast, but who's arguing? Baguette is specified here because it lends a little crunch and chewiness to proceedings, but slices of brioche or white bread also work well. Just make sure the slices are in a single layer in the roasting tray.

unsalted butter, for greasing
4 large eggs
200ml milk
1½ tsp vanilla extract
1 tsp mixed spice
4 tbsp caster sugar
12 slices of baguette, preferably stale, cut 1.5cm thick on the diagonal
maple syrup, for drizzling

Serves: 4 | Takes: 25 minutes, plus 30 minutes soaking

Generously butter a 30 x 20 x 5-cm roasting tray.

Whisk the eggs, milk, vanilla, mixed spice and sugar together in a shallow bowl.

Dip the bread slices into the egg mixture, giving both sides a really good soak. Transfer to the prepared roasting tray in a single layer – the slices should fit snugly. Pour over any remaining egg mixture and leave to soak for 30 minutes, turning over the bread slices halfway through. Meanwhile, preheat the oven to 200°C/400°F.

Bake for 15 minutes, or until the bread is puffed and golden. Serve hot, drizzled with maple syrup.

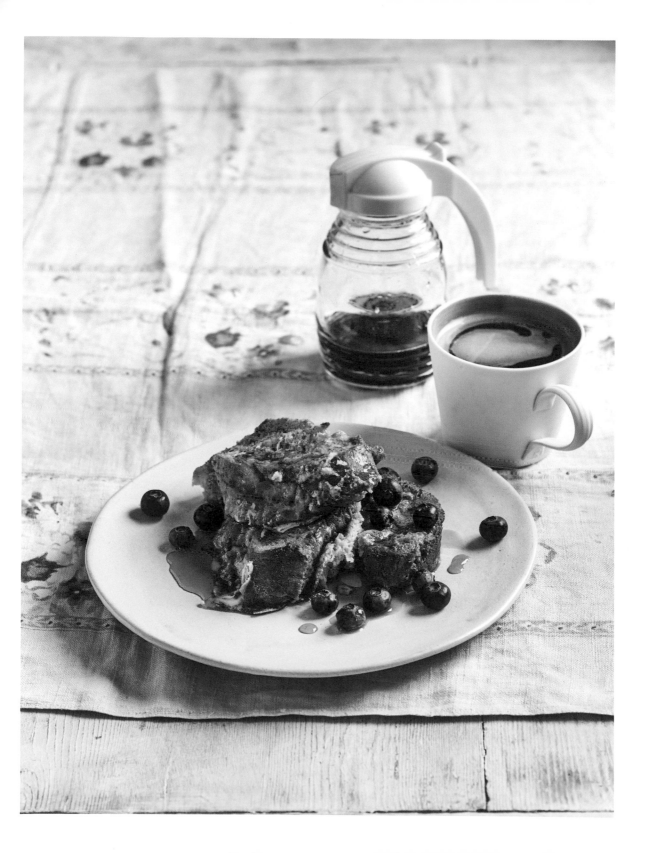

Berry and banana breakfast traybake

Oats, nuts, fruit and yoghurt – sounds like breakfast, but tastes like afternoon tea, so what's not to like? There might be a lot of ingredients here but it's incredibly easy to pull together and results in an ultra-moist and flavourful breakfast that's portable if you need it to be.

180g plain flour
90g porridge oats
60g golden caster sugar
1 tsp baking powder
1 tsp bicarbonate of soda
¼ tsp fine sea salt
1½ tsp ground cinnamon
50g raisins
30g pecan nuts, roughly chopped
2 large ripe bananas
2 large eggs
200g Greek yoghurt
1 tsp vanilla extract
finely grated zest of ½ lemon
5 tbsp mild olive oil
100g blueberries
1–2 tbsp dark brown soft sugar

Makes: 12 squares | Takes: 40 minutes

Preheat the oven to 180°C/350°F. Butter a 30 x 20 x 5-cm roasting tray and line with baking parchment.

Whisk the flour, oats, sugar, baking powder, bicarbonate of soda, salt and cinnamon together in a mixing bowl. Stir in the raisins and pecans.

Mash the bananas with a fork in a jug until sloppy, then add the remaining ingredients, except the blueberries and dark brown sugar, and mix well.

Stir the wet ingredients into the dry until just combined – some lumps and small bits of dry ingredients are fine. Pour into the prepared roasting tray and smooth the top with a spatula. Scatter the blueberries evenly over the top and push them gently into batter – you don't want them to disappear, just half buried. Sprinkle over the brown sugar.

Bake for 25 minutes, or until golden and an inserted skewer comes out clean. Cut into 12 squares and serve warm or cold.

Classic full English breakfast

There are no bells or whistles here, and deliberately so. Some mornings demand a simple hearty breakfast that requires next to no effort – and this is it. Make the tea, read the papers and let the oven do the cooking: just attend to the roasting tray now and then.

olive oil, for brushing
4 good-quality sausages of your choice
8 chestnut mushrooms
sea salt and freshly ground black pepper
4 smoked back bacon rashers
8 cherry tomatoes
2 slices of sourdough bread
2 large eggs

Serves: 2 | Takes: about 35 minutes

Preheat the oven to 240°C/475°F. Lightly brush a 30 x 20 x 5-cm roasting tray with olive oil and place in the oven to heat.

Place the sausages and mushrooms in the hot tray, and shake to lightly coat in the hot oil. Season with salt and pepper and roast for 6 minutes, shaking the tray halfway through.

Reduce the oven temperature to 200°C/400°F. Add the bacon, tomatoes and bread slices, then season with more salt and pepper and shake the tray again. Roast for 20 minutes, shaking the tray and turning the bread over halfway through.

Make 2 spaces in the middle of the ingredients and crack in the eggs. Return to the oven for 6–8 minutes, or until the eggs are done to your liking. Serve immediately.

Potato, chorizo and mushroom hash with chilli mayo

Hearty, spicy and warming, this is a restorative breakfast of the highest order. If you feel inclined, throw in some finely sliced greens like chard or spinach when you return the chorizo to the tray for the final 5 minutes.

240g chorizo sausage (not cooking chorizo)
splash of olive oil
600g potatoes, unpeeled, cut into 2-cm cubes
sea salt and freshly ground black pepper
140g chestnut mushrooms, finely sliced

For the chilli mayo:
90g good-quality mayonnaise
1 tbsp chipotle paste or other chilli paste, or more to taste
squeeze of lime juice
splash of olive oil, to loosen

Serves: 2 generously | Takes: 50 minutes

Preheat the oven to 200°C/400°F. Cut the chorizo into 1-cm coins, then cut each coin in half. Place in a 30 x 20 x 5-cm roasting tray, drizzle over a little olive oil and roast for 10 minutes until it starts to crisp at the edges and release its spicy oil.

Scoop the chorizo out of the tray with a slotted spoon and transfer to a bowl, leaving the spicy oil in the tray. Add the potatoes to the tray, season with salt and pepper and toss well to coat. Roast for 20 minutes, shaking the pan occasionally.

Add the mushrooms to the roasting tray, toss in the oil and roast for a further 10 minutes. Return the chorizo to the tray and roast for a final 5 minutes.

Meanwhile, stir all the ingredients for the chilli mayonnaise together in a bowl to combine.

Serve the hash hot with the chilli mayonnaise spooned over.

Baked apple porridge with chia seeds, raisins and macadamia nuts

Why stand at the stove stirring a porridge pot when you can toss the ingredients in a roasting tray and go back to bed for 30 minutes while it cooks? This is porridge as it should be: creamy and brimming with the flavour of apples, cinnamon and nuts.

unsalted butter, for greasing
200g rolled oats
2 tbsp chia seeds
2 eating apples, peeled, cored and
    chopped into small cubes
70g raisins
70g macadamia nuts or blanched
    hazelnuts, roughly chopped
2 tsp ground cinnamon
½ tsp fine sea salt
300ml milk
3 tbsp runny honey
light brown soft sugar, for sprinkling

To serve (optional):
yoghurt or milk
fresh fruit of choice

Serves: 6 | Takes: 40 minutes

Preheat the oven to 160°C/325°F. Lightly butter a 30 x 20 x 5-cm roasting tray.

Stir the oats, chia seeds, apples, raisins, nuts, cinnamon and salt together in a large bowl. Stir in 350ml boiling water, the milk and honey. Pour the mixture into the prepared tray and bake for 30 minutes.

Remove the tray from the oven and stir the porridge thoroughly, adding a splash more water if needed to produce the desired thickness. Sprinkle over the sugar and bake for a further 5 minutes. Serve hot with yoghurt or milk and some fresh fruit, if you like.

Oat and buckwheat granola

The buckwheat flakes give this a slightly nutty, somehow more grown-up flavour than granola made solely with oats as the base – but it's not too overpowering.

150g rolled oats
50g buckwheat flakes
90g mixed nuts, such as almonds, pistachios, pecans and macadamia nuts, roughly chopped
30g mixed seeds
¼ tsp fine sea salt
1 tsp ground cinnamon
1 tbsp vegetable oil
4 tbsp maple syrup
1 tbsp runny honey
1 tsp vanilla extract
80g mixed dried fruit of choice, chopped
15g desiccated coconut

Makes: 420g | Serves 4–6
Takes: 1 hour 15 minutes

Preheat the oven to 150°C/300°F and line a 30 x 20 x 5-cm roasting tray with baking parchment. Add the oats, buckwheat flakes, nuts, seeds, salt and cinnamon to the tray and stir well to combine.

Mix the vegetable oil, maple syrup, honey and vanilla together in a jug, then pour over the oat mixture. Stir until the dry ingredients are coated – you might think there's not enough liquid but keep mixing until everything looks slightly damp.

Spread the mixture out in the tray and bake for 50 minutes, until lightly golden, shaking the tray regularly. The granola will crisp up as it cools.

Transfer the mixture to a large bowl, add the dried fruit and coconut and mix until evenly distributed. Allow to cool before storing in an airtight container for up to 1 month.

Baked ruby grapefruit with spices and brown sugar

Grilled grapefruit is a breakfast classic, but this recipe rings some changes. Baking instead of grilling softens the whole fruit rather than just the top, coaxing out the juices and mellowing the delicious tartness. Cutting the grapefruit into segments before cooking allows the sugar to seep right through and makes eating it easier, of course.

1 ruby grapefruit
2 generous pinches of ground cinnamon
2 generous pinches of ground ginger
2 heaped tsp Demerara sugar
Greek yoghurt, to serve

Serves: 2 | Takes: 15 minutes

Preheat the oven to 220°C/425°F. Cut the grapefruit in half across the equator. Cut between the flesh and the white pith of each half with a small, serrated knife, working at an angle to reach the bottom of the fruit. Slice along the membranes.

Place the grapefruit halves, cut-side up, in a 30 x 20 x 5-cm roasting tray and sprinkle over the cinnamon, ginger, then the sugar.

Bake for 10 minutes until the sugar has melted. Serve immediately with Greek yoghurt.

Quick croque madame

A truly authentic croque boasts a layer of creamy béchamel sauce, but this is equally tasty – and saves you a good amount of cooking and washing up. It makes a perfect breakfast or brunch – just scale up the recipe according to the number of mouths to feed. A 30 x 20 x 5-cm roasting tray should fit 4–6 croques.

olive oil, for brushing
salted butter, for buttering
1 large slice of sourdough or country-
    style bread
good-quality mayonnaise or Dijon
    mustard or both, for spreading
1 large thick slice of ham
1 large egg
40g grated Gruyère cheese

Makes: 1 | Takes: 20 minutes

Preheat the oven to 200°C/400°F and lightly brush a 30 x 20 x 5-cm roasting tray with olive oil.

Generously butter both sides of the bread. Stamp a circle out of the centre of the bread using a cutter or eggcup a little larger than an egg yolk. Spread the top of the bread with mayonnaise and/or mustard.

Place the bread and the stamped out circle in the tray. Top the bread with the ham – you will have to cut it so it doesn't cover the hole.

Carefully crack the egg into the hole so that it holds the yolk. Scatter the cheese over the top so that the bread, ham and egg are covered.

Bake for 12–15 minutes, or until the cheese has melted, the egg white is set and the yolk is still a little gooey. Serve immediately.

Cheese and bacon swirls

Rolling out of bed and straight into a baking session might not sound appealing, but honestly this is so easy. The tiny effort involved in wrapping pastry around bacon and cheese will be amply rewarded, and beats an early-morning trip to the shops for pastries.

1 sheet ready-rolled puff pastry,
    or 320g block pastry
plain flour, for dusting
125g grated Cheddar cheese
120g bacon, chopped into small pieces
1 spring onion, finely chopped
1 large egg, lightly beaten

Makes: 12 | Takes: 40 minutes,
    plus 20 minutes chilling

Preheat the oven to 180°C/350°F and line a 30 x 20 x 5-cm roasting tray with baking parchment.

Lay the pastry sheet on a lightly floured work surface or, if using a block, roll out into a 25 x 30-cm rectangle. Scatter over the cheese, bacon and spring onion. Roll the pastry from the short end into a tight log and chill in the fridge for 20 minutes.

Cut the log into 12 equal slices and arrange them cut-side up and spaced apart in the prepared roasting tray. Press them down to flatten a little, then brush the tops with beaten egg.

Bake for 25–30 minutes, or until puffed and golden. Serve warm.

Snacks
+
Light Bites

Parmesan, garlic and poppy seed crackers

These delicious salty bites go perfectly with drinks – much nicer than a bowl of crisps. Don't be tempted to cook them for longer than suggested, as not much stands between perfectly cooked and burnt. A tip for garlic granules that (inevitably, it seems) clump together: pop a chunk in a mortar and pound with a pestle to make a powder.

60g finely grated Parmesan cheese
½ tsp poppy seeds
¼ tsp garlic granules

Makes: about 12 | Takes: 15 minutes

Preheat the oven to 180°C/350°F and line a 30 x 20 x 5-cm roasting tray with baking parchment.

Mix all the ingredients together in a bowl. Place 1 level tbsp of the mixture in the prepared tray in equally spaced mounds. Flatten with the back of a spoon to make discs, about 6cm wide. Bake for 7 minutes, or until just turning pale gold at the edges.

Leave in the tray for 2 minutes, then transfer to kitchen paper with a spatula to cool and crisp up. Store in an airtight container for up to 2 days.

Baked figs, halloumi, prosciutto and basil

It's quite easy for one person to put away a whole tray of these; the combination of salty ham and melted cheese with the sweet figs is heavenly, especially served hot from the oven. Serve them as a lovely starter with a few bitter salad leaves, or a decadent bite with drinks.

olive oil, for greasing and drizzling
180g halloumi cheese
12 large basil leaves
6 large ripe figs, halved lengthways
12 long slices of prosciutto ham, about 100g
1 tbsp runny honey, or to taste (optional)

Makes: 12 | Takes: 15 minutes

Preheat the oven to 200°C/400°F and lightly oil a 30 x 20 x 5-cm roasting tray.

Cut the halloumi into six 5-mm slices, then cut each slice in half to make 12 small rectangles.

Fold a basil leaf in half, place it on the cut side of a fig half and top with a piece of halloumi. Wrap in a piece of prosciutto and transfer to the roasting tray. Repeat.

Drizzle with olive oil and roast for 10 minutes, or until the prosciutto is starting to crisp up and the halloumi is hot. Serve immediately, drizzled with honey, if you like.

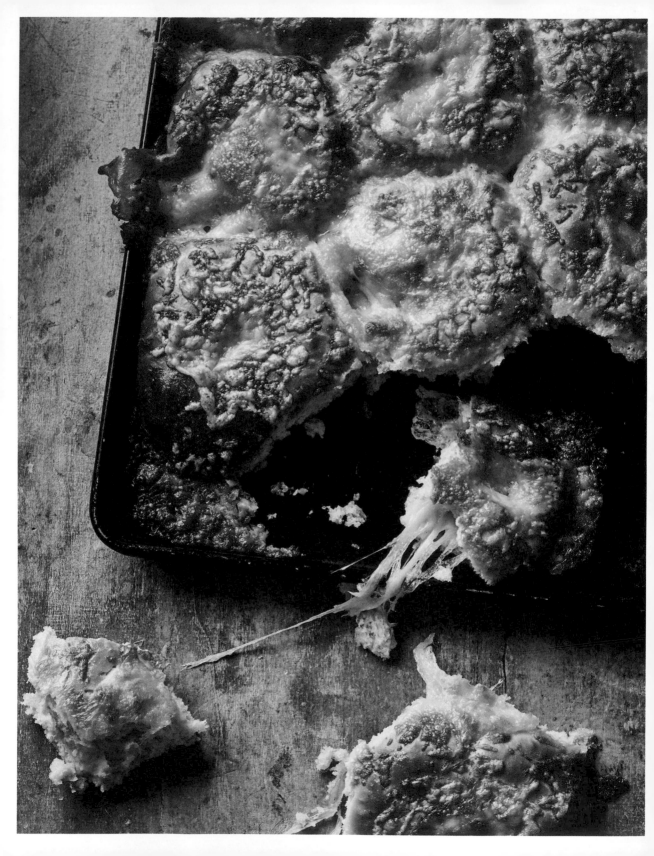

Massively cheesy cheese and garlic pull-apart rolls

Pulling these rolls apart is one thing; tearing yourself away from the vicinity of the tray is a trickier task entirely. Loads of cheese, garlic and bread together in a group hug – there's nothing more to say.

120g unsalted butter, softened
4 garlic cloves, crushed
500g strong white bread flour, plus extra for dusting
1 tbsp caster sugar
1 tsp sea salt
20g fast-action dried yeast
320ml milk
240g fresh mozzarella cheese, cut into 12 equal chunks, plus an extra 130g, chopped
1 large egg, lightly beaten
140g grated strong Cheddar cheese

Makes: 12 | Takes: 40 minutes, plus 20 minutes resting

Preheat the oven to 200°C/400°F. Mix the butter and garlic together in a small bowl. Transfer the butter to a 30 x 20 x 5-cm roasting tray and place inside the oven for a few minutes to melt – don't let the garlic colour.

Combine the flour, sugar, salt and yeast together in a large mixing bowl. Make a well in the centre and pour in the milk and warm garlic butter from the roasting tray. Make sure you scrape all the garlic into the bowl. Mix until everything comes together into a rough dough. Set aside for 10 minutes covered with a clean cloth. Meanwhile, brush the residual butter left in the tray up the sides.

Knead the dough on a lightly floured work surface for 10 minutes, or for 8 minutes in an electric mixer with a dough hook attachment. It should be soft and elastic and come away easily from the work surface or the sides of the bowl. Divide into 12 pieces, roughly 75g each, and roll into balls.

Press a ball into a 10-cm disc on a lightly floured surface. Place a mozzarella chunk in the centre, bring the dough up over the cheese and pinch the edges together to seal tightly. Turn over and shape into a ball. Repeat with the rest of dough and mozzarella. Arrange the balls in the roasting tray to make three rows of four equally spaced apart. Cover with a clean cloth and leave for 10 minutes.

Brush the tops of the rolls with the beaten egg, then tuck the remaining mozzarella and the Cheddar cheese into the gaps. Bake for 20 minutes until risen and golden.

Ricotta, asparagus and mint tartlets

The lemon and mint makes these tartlets sing: they're a perfect springtime lunch or starter when tender asparagus is in season and at its very best. Serve with a good mixed salad.

80g ricotta cheese
2 heaped tbsp finely grated
    Parmesan cheese
1 large egg, beaten
grated zest of ½ lemon
½ tbsp olive oil, plus extra for drizzling
1 tbsp chopped mint, plus extra for
    sprinkling
sea salt and freshly ground black pepper
1 x 320-g sheet of ready-rolled puff
    pastry or 320g block pastry (keep
    chilled until needed)
24 fine asparagus spears, trimmed to
    about 12cm

Makes: 4 | Takes: 35 minutes

Preheat the oven to 180°C/350°F and line a 30 x 20 x 5-cm roasting tray with baking parchment.

Beat the ricotta, Parmesan, 2 tablespoons of the beaten egg, the lemon zest, olive oil, mint and salt and pepper together in a bowl.

Trim the pastry sheet, or roll out the block, into a 30 x 20-cm rectangle. Cut in half crossways and lengthways to make four 10 x 15-cm rectangles, and transfer to the prepared roasting tray.

Mark a 1-cm border around each pastry rectangle with the tines of a fork and brush the border with the remaining beaten egg. Prick inside the border with the fork. Divide the ricotta mixture between each tartlet and spread out inside the border. Top with the asparagus spears, drizzle with a little olive oil and sprinkle over more mint and salt. Bake for 25 minutes, or until puffed and golden.

Serve immediately.

Roast buttered almonds with honey and chilli

These are super tasty, take virtually no effort at all and make a lovely snack. An added bonus is that your kitchen will be filled with the wonderful smell of toasted nuts and butter.

3 tbsp unsalted butter
3 tbsp runny honey
1 tsp chilli flakes
200g blanched almonds
sea salt flakes

Makes: a small bowlful
Takes: about 25 minutes

Preheat the oven to 170°C/325°F. Place the butter in a 30 x 20 x 5-cm roasting tray and transfer to the oven for 2 minutes to melt.

Remove the tray from the oven and stir the honey and chilli flakes into the melted butter. Add the almonds and toss to coat, ensuring they are spread out in a single layer.

Roast for 20–25 minutes, or until the nuts are golden – keep an eye on them, as they burn easily, and shake the tray occasionally. Sprinkle with salt. Delicious served warm – the nuts will crisp up as they cool a little.

Tuna, caper and onion mini pies

Blink and they're gone: that's what happens when you make these gorgeous mini pies. There's something about the combination of flavours that make them completely addictive, especially eaten hot, straight out of the oven.

200g canned tuna in oil
    (drained weight)
50g finely chopped onion
20g capers, rinsed, drained and
    finely chopped
½ red pepper, deseeded and
    finely chopped
100g cream cheese
1 tsp smoked paprika
sea salt and freshly ground black pepper
2 sheets of ready-rolled shortcrust pastry,
    about 320g each
1 egg, lightly beaten

Makes: 12 | Takes: 45 minutes

Preheat the oven to 200°C/400°F and line a 30 x 20 x 5-cm roasting tray with baking parchment.

Mix all the ingredients, except the pastry and egg, together in a bowl until completely combined. The cream cheese should bind everything together.

Using a plate or bowl as guide, cut twelve 6-cm circles from the pastry sheets. Lightly brush the edges with a little of the beaten egg. Place equal quantities of the tuna mixture along the centre of each circle – a dessertspoonful is about right. Pick a circle up with your hands, fold it in half and gently press the edges together, then pleat, to seal. Repeat with the remaining pastry and filling, transferring to the roasting tray as you go. Brush the tops with the remaining beaten egg.

Bake for 30–35 minutes until beautifully golden. Eat the pies as soon as they are cool enough to do so safely.

(Pictured overleaf)

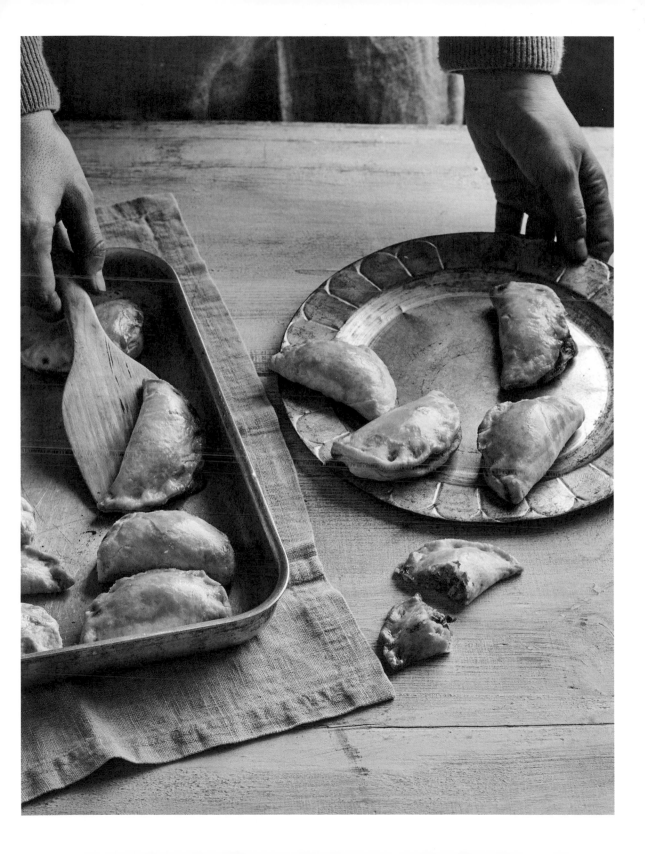

Sweet potato and corn fritters

These are deeeelicious. You could eat them as a side or starter, maybe with a bowl of guacamole alongside, or gobble them hot straight from the roasting tray with a squeeze of lime and a sprinkling of good sea salt flakes.

200g sweet potatoes, grated
100g sweetcorn kernels
   (fresh or from a can)
1 tbsp self-raising flour
1 fat garlic clove, crushed
20g finely grated Parmesan cheese
1 large egg
2 tsp Aleppo pepper (or 2 tsp sweet
   paprika plus a generous pinch of
   cayenne)
½ tsp sea salt

Makes: 8 | Takes: 35 minutes

Preheat the oven to 200°C/400°F and line a 30 x 20 x 5-cm roasting tray with baking parchment.

Place all the ingredients in a bowl and mix well. Drop 8 equal mounds of the mixture into the prepared roasting tray and flatten them slightly with a fork.

Roast for 25 minutes, or until they are starting to crisp up at the edges and can be easily flipped with a spatula. Turn over and roast for a further 5 minutes. Serve immediately.

Potato rösti with smoked ham and eggs

Just a handful of humble ingredients come together here for a joyous lunch (or even breakfast) that's far easier to make in a roasting tray than in a frying pan. As ever, keep your eyes glued to the eggs as they bake: all ovens are different and you want the yolks to spill their loveliness over the rösti when you cut into them, not require a carving knife.

3 tbsp duck or goose fat, or olive oil
4 medium waxy potatoes,
    about 180g each
4 thick slices of smoked ham,
    about 40g each, chopped
sea salt flakes and freshly ground
    black pepper
4 large eggs

Makes: 4 | Takes: about 45 minutes

Preheat the oven to 200°C/400°F. Place the fat or olive oil in a 30 x 20 x 5-cm roasting tray to melt and/or get hot.

Grate the potatoes into a bowl – you can peel them if you like, but the skin adds flavour. Add the ham, season with salt and pepper and mix well.

Spoon 4 mounds of potato into the prepared roasting tray, and gently spread into circles, about 1.5cm high. Spoon a little of the hot fat or oil over the top of each one. Roast for 30 minutes, or until golden at the edges and beginning to turn brown on top.

Make an indentation in each rösti with the back of a soup spoon and crack in an egg. Return to the oven for a further 6–8 minutes, or until the whites are just set and the yolks are still runny. Serve immediately.

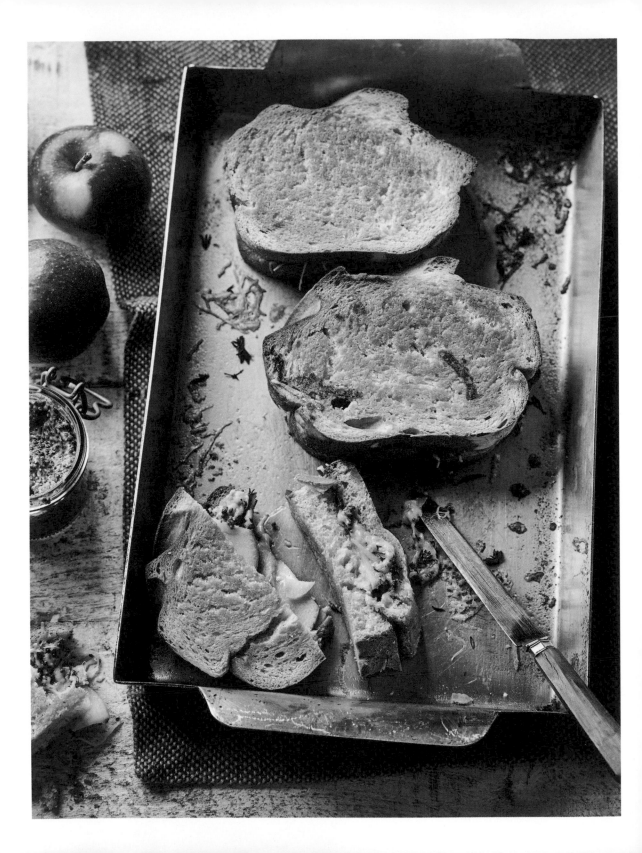

Cheese toasties with apple, thyme and mustard

There's nothing wrong with simple toasted cheese, of course, but the addition of apple or pear and fragrant herbs elevates this iconic snack to something gorgeous. It's lovely to have a mix of cheese: Comté or Gruyère for gooeyness and strong Cheddar for punchy flavour.

oil, for greasing
salted butter, for spreading
2 slices of bloomer or other white bread
Dijon or seedy mustard, for spreading
25g grated Gruyère cheese, Comté or mozzarella cheese
25g grated mature Cheddar or other flavourful cheese
½ apple or pear, finely sliced
about ¼ tsp chopped thyme leaves

Serves: 1 (but can easily be scaled up to make 2–3 in the same tray)
Takes: 15 minutes

Preheat the oven to 220°C/425°F and lightly oil a 30 x 20 x 5-cm roasting tray. Place it in the oven to heat.

Butter the bread on both sides, then spread mustard on one slice. Top the mustardy slice with the cheeses, apple or pear and thyme. Place the other bread slice on top and press together.

Place the sandwich in the hot roasting tray and place a baking tray or ovenproof pan on top – this will press the toasty together like a panini. Bake for 10 minutes, or until the top and the bottom of the sandwich are golden and the cheese melted. Serve immediately.

Tortilla chips with garlic and chipotle salt

This is unashamedly a cheat's version of those addictive bagged snacks that turn your fingers fluorescent orange. These tortillas are fresher, tastier and healthier, as they're not deep-fried. The golden rule is to watch the chips like a hawk, as they burn in a flash.

1 good-quality corn tortilla per batch
1 tsp garlic flavoured olive oil, or
    plain is fine
sea salt flakes
chipotle powder or smoked paprika
garlic granules

Makes: 8 chips per batch
Takes: 10 minutes per batch

Preheat the oven to 180°C/350°F.

Lightly brush the tortilla on both sides with oil, making sure you brush right up to the edges. Using a pizza cutter or sharp knife, cut into 8 equal pieces. Arrange in a single layer in a 30 x 20 x 5-cm roasting tray and bake for 5–6 minutes, turning over halfway through. They will crisp up more as they cool.

While the chips are hot, sprinkle with salt, chipotle powder or paprika and garlic granules.

Lamb, pistachio and mint sausage rolls

Who doesn't love a sausage roll? Spiced meat encased in buttery puff pastry, eaten warm and dunked in ketchup, with a cold drink on the side, is one of life's absolute pleasures.

500g minced lamb
½ onion, grated
25g chopped pistachio nuts
1 tbsp chipotle paste
15g chopped mint leaves
2 garlic cloves, crushed
sea salt and freshly ground black pepper
1 x 320-g sheet of ready-rolled puff
   pastry or 320g block pastry
plain flour, for dusting
1 large egg, lightly beaten

Makes: 12 small sausage rolls
Takes: 50 minutes

Preheat the oven to 220°C/425°F and line a 30 x 20 x 5-cm roasting tray with baking parchment.

Place the lamb, onion, pistachios, chipotle paste, mint and garlic in a bowl. Season generously with salt and pepper and mix well with your hands until everything is combined.

Roll out the pastry sheet or block on a lightly floured work surface into a square roughly 36 x 36cm. Fold the pastry in half, lightly press to make a crease, then unfold and cut along the line to make 2 rectangles, 36 x 18cm.

Place half the meat mixture down the centre of one of the rectangles of pastry in a sausage shape. Brush the edges of the pastry with a little of the beaten egg, then firmly roll it up and seal well. Repeat with the remaining lamb mixture and pastry rectangle. Seal the rolls well.

Trim the ends, then cut each pastry log into 6 equal pieces. Make a couple of slits in the top of each piece and transfer to the prepared roasting tray.

Brush the tops of the sausage rolls with the remaining beaten egg and bake for 25 minutes until puffed and golden. Serve warm.

Crispy chicken scratchings

These are a bit naughty: chicken skin bites baked to salty crispness. Ask your butcher for the skins, or remove them from chicken breasts, drumsticks and thighs.

250g chicken skin
sea salt flakes

Makes: 1 bowlful | Takes: 30 minutes

Preheat the oven to 180°C/350°F.

Cut the chicken skin into pieces, roughly 4-cm square – the exact size doesn't matter, so long as they're equal and not too small. Place in a single layer in a 30 x 20 x 5-cm roasting tray and sprinkle with salt.

Bake for about 30 minutes, shaking the tray every 10 minutes and pouring out the rendered fat each time (save it to use instead of oil or duck fat in another dish).

Tip the scratchings onto kitchen paper, sprinkle with a little more salt if needed, and serve immediately.

Pizza bianca

This is such glorious pizza: garlicky, chewy and simple. Adorn with anything you fancy – curls of wafer-thin prosciutto and cheese are delicious. Or serve with a bowl of good extra virgin olive oil on the side for dunking, and a bowl of olives.

500g strong white bread flour,
   plus extra for dusting (optional)
1½ tsp fast-action dried yeast
1½ tsp sea salt
2 tbsp olive oil, plus extra for oiling
   and drizzling
cornflour, for dusting
sea salt flakes
2 large rosemary sprigs, leaves removed
   and chopped

Makes: 2 pizzas | Takes: 40 minutes,
   plus 3 hours rising

Using an electric mixer or a mixing bowl, whisk the flour, yeast and salt together. Stir in 350ml warm water and the olive oil. Use a dough hook to knead for 5–8 minutes, or turn onto a lightly floured surface and knead by hand for 10 minutes, until smooth and elastic. Place in an oiled bowl, cover with clingfilm and leave to rise in a warm place for 2 hours.

Punch down the dough, divide into 2 equal pieces and roll into sausages. Lightly flour the work surface with cornflour and leave the dough to rest on it covered with a clean cloth for 1 hour. After 30 minutes, preheat the oven to its highest setting and place a 30 x 20 x 5-cm roasting tray inside to heat.

Cut out a piece of baking parchment, 30 x 20cm, and place a piece of dough in the middle. Stretch and press the dough out with your fingertips to cover the paper – it should be nice and dimpled. Carefully transfer the dough and paper to the hot roasting tray, sprinkle generously with salt and half the rosemary and drizzle with olive oil.

Bake for 12–15 minutes until the crust is golden with a few dark spots. Serve hot from the oven and repeat with the remaining dough.

(Pictured overleaf)

Garlicky mushroom and thyme tartines

Tartine is a posh name for loaded toast, and this one makes an excellent light lunch. A mixture of mushrooms, including wild ones, would be perfect, but large Portobellos or flat caps on their own work nicely.

extra virgin olive oil, for brushing
   and drizzling
120g mixed mushrooms
50g unsalted butter, softened
20g grated Parmesan cheese
1 garlic clove, crushed
1 heaped tsp finely chopped thyme
finely grated zest of ½ lemon
sea salt and freshly ground black pepper
2 large slices of sourdough or good-
   quality country-style bread

Makes: 2 large tartines
Takes: 25 minutes

Preheat the oven to 220°C/425°F and brush a 30 x 20 x 5-cm roasting tray with olive oil.

Finely chop half the mushrooms and place in a medium bowl. Add the butter, Parmesan, garlic, thyme, lemon zest and salt and pepper. Mix until well combined and roughly spreadable.

Spread equal amounts of the mixture over the bread slices and transfer to the roasting tray.

Slice the remaining mushrooms into bite-sized pieces and arrange on top of the mushroom mixture. Drizzle with olive oil and season with salt and pepper.

Roast for 15 minutes, or until the mushrooms are tender and the bottom of the bread is crisp and golden. Serve hot.

Lunch
+
Warm Salads

Spinach, bacon and double cheese bake

Something magical happens when eggs, cream, cheese, smoky bacon and vegetables are united. This dish is lovely served with a crisp green salad and also fab popped in lunchboxes the next day, if there's any left over.

3 medium waxy potatoes, about 400g, peeled and cut into 2-cm cubes
1 red onion, quartered, layers separated
1 tbsp extra virgin olive oil
sea salt and freshly ground black pepper
150g smoked bacon lardons
8 large eggs, lightly beaten
240ml double cream
50g grated Parmesan cheese
130g grated mozzarella cheese
70g spinach leaves, finely sliced
2 garlic cloves, crushed
1 tsp sea salt flakes

Serves: 6 | Takes: 1 hour

Preheat the oven to 200°C/400°F.

Place the potatoes and onion in a 30 x 20 x 5-cm roasting tray, toss with the olive oil and season with salt and pepper. Roast for 15 minutes, shaking the tray occasionally. Add the lardons to the tray, shake well and roast for a further 10 minutes.

Meanwhile, stir the eggs and cream together in a large bowl. Stir in the cheeses, spinach, garlic, the 1 teaspoon of sea salt flakes and some pepper and mix well.

When the vegetables and lardons have done their time in the oven, loosen them with a spatula to ensure they're not sticking to the bottom of the tray. Pour in the egg mixture and use a wooden spoon to nudge the vegetables around so they're evenly distributed and the spinach is almost submerged in the liquid. Bake for 20–25 minutes, or until puffed and golden and the eggs are just set. Let the tray stand for 5 minutes before cutting into squares to serve.

Baked whole camembert with rosemary, honey and garlic toast

This is so lovely and decadent, with the warm gooey interior perfect for dunking with crunchy, garlicky spears of toast. It's very easy to eat a whole one yourself, but share if you have to.

2 garlic cloves
4 slices of sourdough bread or similar
extra virgin olive oil, for drizzling
1 whole Camembert, about 250g
1 tsp runny honey, plus extra to serve
8 rosemary tips

Optional extras for dunking:
gherkins
Parma ham
sliced fruit, such as figs, pears or apples

Serves: 1–2 | Takes: 20 minutes

Preheat the oven to 200°C/400°F.

Cut one of the garlic cloves in half and rub on both sides of the bread with the cut side. Drizzle both sides with olive oil and place in a 30 x 20 x 5-cm roasting tray.

Take the cheese out of its box, remove the paper wrapping and return it to the box. (If the cheese doesn't come in a box, place in a small baking pot.) Cut four long deep slashes in the cheese, and spoon in the honey.

Cut the remaining garlic into slivers, including what's left of the clove used to rub the bread, and poke into the slashes. Poke the rosemary tips in, too. Drizzle with olive oil and place in the roasting tray alongside the bread.

Bake for 15 minutes until the cheese is bubbling and the bread toasted and golden. Serve immediately with any optional extras for dunking.

Spicy cheese and bacon burgers

It's fair to say these don't have the charred exterior of burgers cooked on the grill – but what they can boast is a tender, juicy interior that's absolutely packed with flavour. No dried-out burgers in this roasting tray.

olive oil, for brushing
500g beef mince, ideally 20% fat
2 smoked bacon rashers, finely chopped
1 tbsp sriracha sauce (if you have none, or don't like spice, tomato ketchup is fine)
sea salt flakes and freshly ground black pepper
1 large onion, finely sliced
4 Monterey Jack or Gouda cheese slices
4 burger buns, toasted if you like
sliced tomatoes and lettuce, to serve

Serves: 4 | Takes: 30 minutes

Preheat the oven to 180°C/350°F and brush a 30 x 20 x 5-cm roasting tray with olive oil.

Place the mince, bacon, sriracha and salt and pepper in a bowl and mix with your hands until everything is well combined. Shape the mixture into four equal-sized patties, about 1.5cm high – don't pack them too tightly, just enough to keep their shape.

Spread the onion out in the tray and place the burgers on top. Roast for about 15 minutes, flipping halfway through. Top each burger with a cheese slice and roast for a further 5 minutes. The burger should feel slightly springy to touch.

Serve the burgers and onions stuffed between the buns with some tomato and lettuce.

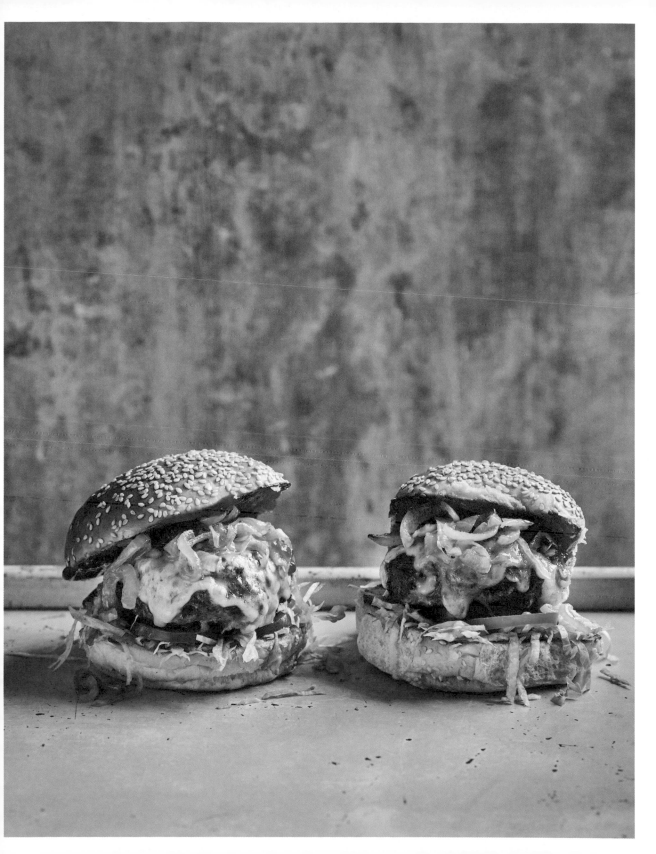

Chicken fajitas

There's something universally appealing about a self-assembly meal. This version is the simplest of all – a whack-it-all-in-the-tray affair that barely constitutes cooking. And it's really tasty.

For the chicken:
3 boneless and skinless chicken breasts, cut into thin strips
1 large red pepper, cut into thin strips
1 tbsp smoked paprika
1 tsp ground cumin
2 tsp dried oregano
1 tsp cayenne pepper or chilli powder
juice of 1 lime
2 tbsp olive oil

For the salsa:
1 bunch of coriander
1 fat garlic clove, crushed
2 large ripe tomatoes
juice of ½ lime, plus extra to taste
3 tbsp extra virgin olive oil

corn tortilla wraps, to serve

Optional toppings including:
grated Cheddar cheese, guacamole, shredded lettuce, crème fraîche

Serves: 4 | Takes: 35 minutes

Preheat the oven to 200°C/400°F and place a 30 x 20 x 5-cm roasting tray or dish inside to heat.

Place all the chicken ingredients in a bowl and toss with your hands until everything is coated in a slick of spiced oil. Set aside for 5 minutes.

Meanwhile, roughly chop the coriander leaves and tender stems and place in a bowl with the remaining salsa ingredients. Set aside.

Tip the chicken into the hot roasting tray. Roast for 20–25 minutes, shaking the tray occasionally, until the chicken is cooked through.

Serve wrapped in tortillas with the tomato salsa and your choice of toppings.

Fish and chips

The precise cooking time for the fish will depend on its thickness, but choose reasonably chunky fillets, or the crumb coating won't have time to crisp up and turn golden.

400g large floury potatoes, such as Maris Piper, Desirée or Russets
1 tbsp rapeseed oil, plus extra for drizzling
celery salt, herb salt or plain sea salt
2 cod, hake, plaice or other white fish fillets, about 120g each, cut into 4-cm strips
40g plain flour
1 large egg, lightly beaten
50g panko breadcrumbs
20g golden breadcrumbs
½ tsp smoked paprika
fine sea salt and freshly ground black pepper

Serves: 2 | Takes: 45 minutes

Preheat the oven to its maximum temperature. Place a 30 x 20 x 5-cm roasting tray inside to heat. Have ready a wire rack that sits in or over the roasting tray.

Cut the potatoes into chips about 1cm thick (peel them if you like, but the skin adds flavour). Transfer to a bowl of cold water as you go. Drain well and pat dry with kitchen paper. Return to the bowl, add the oil and salt and toss to coat. Carefully arrange in a single layer in the hot roasting tray. Roast for 15 minutes, shaking the tray occasionally.

Meanwhile, place the flour, egg and breadcrumbs in three separate shallow bowls. Stir the paprika into the flour and generously season with salt and pepper. Dredge the fish strips in the flour, then the egg and finally the breadcrumbs, pressing the breadcrumbs to encourage them to stick. Transfer to the wire rack and drizzle with oil.

When the chips have done their 15 minutes, flip them over with a spatula and reduce the oven temperature to 220°C/425°F. Sit the fish on its rack in or on the roasting tray and roast for about 20 minutes, or until the fish is cooked through and breadcrumbs are pale golden. Serve.

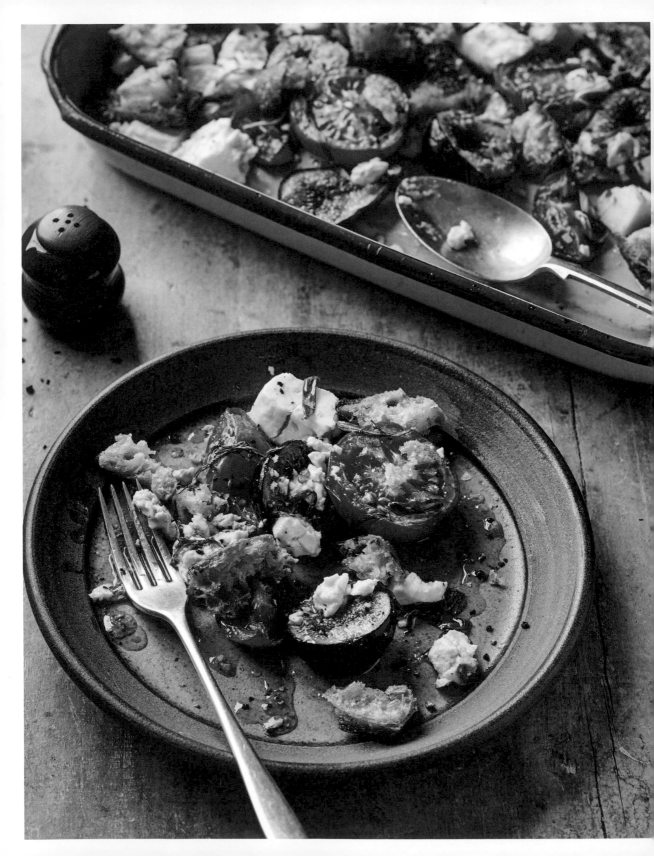

Warm salad of roast tomatoes, figs and feta with tarragon

You could replace half the tomatoes with a handful of mixed cherry tomatoes to add extra colour and variety to this lovely salad.

6 medium tomatoes
6 fresh figs, stalks trimmed off
   and halved
250g feta cheese, broken into
   large chunks
250g sourdough bread, torn into chunks
3 tarragon stalks, leaves removed
extra virgin olive oil, for drizzling
sea salt flakes and freshly ground
   black pepper
squeeze of lemon, to serve

Serves: 4–6 | Takes: 30 minutes

Preheat the oven to 180°C/350°F.

Cut half the tomatoes in half and the remainder into quarters, and place in a 30 x 20 x 5-cm roasting tray. Add the figs, feta, bread and tarragon, drizzle generously with olive oil and season with salt and pepper. Gently tumble everything together.

Roast for 25 minutes, shaking the tray occasionally, until the tomatoes and figs have collapsed down a little and released some of their juices, and the feta is golden at the edges.

Serve warm with a squeeze of lemon and more salt and pepper if needed.

Maple and lime-roasted squash with lentils, ricotta and basil oil

Fragrant and filling, this makes a sublime meat-free feast on a crisp autumnal day. The sweet comforting flavours of the mushrooms and squash work beautifully with the sprightly herb oil.

750g peeled and deseeded butternut squash, cut into 3-cm chunks
3 tbsp olive oil, plus extra if needed and for drizzling
1 tbsp maple syrup
sea salt and freshly ground black pepper
2 bay leaves
250g cooked green lentils (canned lentils work well)
¾ tsp chilli flakes
finely grated zest of 1 lime
200g mixed mushrooms, such as Portobello or chestnut, cut into thick slices
1 whole ricotta, about 250g

For the basil oil:
20g basil leaves and fine stalks
3 tbsp lime juice (from the lime used for the zest)
2 garlic cloves
120ml extra virgin olive oil

Serves: 4 | Takes: 1 hour

Preheat the oven to 220°C/425°F.

Place the squash in a 30 x 20 x 5-cm roasting tray, drizzle with half the olive oil and all the maple syrup. Season with salt and pepper and toss to coat. Tuck the bay leaves into the tray and roast for 15 minutes.

While the squash is roasting, place the lentils in a small bowl and stir in the remaining olive oil, the chilli flakes, lime zest and salt and pepper. Add to the tray with the squash, then add the mushrooms. Toss to combine, ensuring everything is lightly slicked with oil – add a little more oil if necessary.

Make space in the middle of the tray, add the ricotta and drizzle with oil. Roast for 35–40 minutes, or until the top of the ricotta is golden. Stir the lentils, squash and mushrooms occasionally to prevent them sticking and drying out.

Meanwhile, make the basil oil by blitzing all the ingredients in a food processor or pounding in a mortar with a pestle.

To serve, divide the ricotta, vegetables and lentils among serving plates and generously drizzle with the basil oil.

Warm salad of red cabbage, grapes and halloumi

This is an unusual but tasty winter salad – the cooked grapes provide a pop of sweetness that works beautifully with the salty cheese and earthy cabbage.

100g black seedless grapes,
    halved if large
160g red cabbage, finely sliced
100g halloumi cheese, cut
    into small cubes
20g pumpkin seeds
2 tbsp balsamic vinegar
5 tbsp olive oil
sea salt and freshly ground black pepper
1½ tbsp lime juice, plus extra to taste
½ tsp runny honey
generous pinch of chilli flakes
handful of rocket, about 20g
5g flat leaf parsley, roughly chopped
5g coriander, roughly chopped

Serves: 2–4 | Takes: 30 minutes

Preheat the oven to 200°C/400°F.

Place the grapes, cabbage, halloumi and pumpkin seeds in a 30 x 20 x 5-cm roasting tray. Pour over the balsamic vinegar and 2 tablespoons of the olive oil, then season with salt and pepper and toss until everything is coated. Roast for 20 minutes or so until the grapes and cabbage are tender.

Meanwhile, whisk the remaining olive oil, the lime juice, honey, chilli flakes and salt and pepper together to make a dressing.

Tip the contents of the roasting tray onto a serving platter. Add the rocket and herbs, and toss with the dressing, adding extra lime juice to taste. Serve immediately.

Creamy baked leeks with apple, thyme and goat's cheese

Leeks, apple, cheese and cream parked in the same roasting tray is a very good thing indeed. This makes a fantastic meal served with a crunchy green salad dressed with a sharp vinaigrette.

1 tbsp unsalted butter, plus extra
    for greasing
500g leeks, trimmed, rinsed and cut into
    1-cm coins
sea salt and freshly ground black pepper
2 tbsp olive oil
1 large egg
200ml single cream
200ml vegetable stock
2 garlic cloves, crushed
100g soft goat's cheese
20g grated Parmesan cheese
small handful of thyme leaves
1 eating apple
150g ciabatta, torn into bite-sized pieces
30g finely grated Cheddar cheese

Serves: 4 | Takes: 1 hour 10 minutes

Preheat the oven to 180°C/350°F and butter a 30 x 20 x 5-cm roasting tray.

Place the leeks in the tray, season generously with salt and pepper and toss with the olive oil. Dot the 1 tablespoon butter over the leeks, add a splash of water and cover tightly with foil. Bake for 30 minutes, shaking the tray occasionally.

Meanwhile, stir all the remaining ingredients, except the apple, ciabatta and Cheddar, together in a jug.

When the leeks are done, peel, quarter and core the apple. Slice each quarter into the roasting tray. Add the ciabatta and toss to combine. Pour over the cream mixture and turn the bread to coat. Sprinkle over the Cheddar and bake for another 30 minutes until golden. Serve immediately.

Crispy potato galettes with rosemary and garlic, and smoked salmon

This makes a glorious lunch, flanked by nothing more than a vibrant green salad. The key to this is slicing the potatoes very thinly – it's possible with a sharp knife but much easier on a mandoline or similar hand-held slicer.

3 tbsp goose or duck fat, or
  unsalted butter
1 fat garlic clove, crushed
400g Charlotte or other waxy potatoes,
  ideally all a similar size
1 tsp chopped rosemary
sea salt flakes

To serve:
2 generous smoked salmon slices
2 tbsp crème fraîche

Serves: 2 | Takes: 1 hour

Preheat the oven to 220°C/425°F. Place the fat in a 30 x 20 x 5-cm roasting tray and transfer to the oven for 2 minutes to melt. Pour the melted fat into a small bowl and stir in the garlic. Brush the residual fat in the tray all over the bottom so it's well covered.

Now make the galettes. Finely slice the potatoes with a mandoline or knife; slice and layer the potatoes in the roasting tray as you go to prevent the potatoes from discolouring. Closely overlap the slices to make a 12-cm circle. Brush with the garlicky butter and sprinkle with rosemary and sea salt flakes. Continue layering – there should be enough potato for each galette to have three layers – until you have used up half the potatoes. Repeat to make a second galette. Brush the tops of the galettes with the melted garlic fat and roast for 30–40 minutes until cooked through and crisp at the edges.

Serve with curls of smoked salmon on top and a spoonful of crème fraîche.

Quick flatbread with spiced lamb and tahini

Even though you're making the dough from scratch, this is very easy and really doesn't take long. Serve with a simple salad of sliced red onion, soaked in water for 10 minutes and then drained, mixed with loads of chopped coriander, lemon juice and extra virgin olive oil.

For the flatbread:
120g plain flour, plus extra for dusting
½ tsp fine sea salt
½ tsp baking powder
1 scant tsp dried oregano
120g Greek yoghurt

For the topping:
100g canned chopped tomatoes
2 tsp tomato purée
3 garlic cloves, crushed
2 tsp Aleppo or Turkish (or other) chilli flakes
handful of chopped flat leaf parsley leaves and fine stalks
finely grated zest of ½ lemon
125g minced lamb
sea salt and freshly ground black pepper
4 tbsp tahini

Serves: 2–4 | Takes: 40 minutes

Preheat the oven to its highest setting. Line a 30 x 20 x 5-cm roasting tray with foil so that it overhangs the short sides and place it in the hot oven.

For the flatbread, whisk the flour, salt, baking powder and oregano together in a mixing bowl. Gradually stir in the yoghurt to make a rough dough. Work the dough with your hands to incorporate the flour at the bottom of the bowl. Knead on a lightly floured work surface for a few minutes until smooth. Cover with a damp cloth and leave to rest.

Meanwhile make the topping. Mix all the ingredients, except the tahini, together in a large bowl with a fork, breaking up the meat as much as possible, so everything is well amalgamated. Set aside.

Roll out the dough on a lightly floured surface to make a rectangle slightly smaller than the roasting tray. Carefully remove the hot tray from the oven and lay the dough inside. Spread the top with the tahini right up to the edges (loosen it with olive oil if necessary – it needs to be spreadable). Scatter the meat mixture over the top, spreading it out and breaking up clumps with a fork.

Bake for 12–15 minutes until the meat is browned and the bottom of the flatbread is slightly golden. Serve immediately.

Triple cheese and broccoli pasta

Here's the thing: this isn't an authentic Italian pasta dish but it doesn't pretend to be. It's just a very easy, super-delicious and hearty meal that's likely to become a favourite. It's worth stressing that fresh pasta – readily available these days in the chiller cabinet of convenience stores and supermarkets – is essential. The dried stuff won't work.

400g fresh tagliatelle (from the chiller cabinet)
120g broccoli, cut into tiny florets, thick stalks grated
80g soft goat's cheese, Brie or blue cheese, chopped small
100g fresh mozzarella cheese, chopped small
25g finely grated Parmesan cheese, plus extra to serve

For the sauce:
300ml whole milk
300ml double cream
3 garlic cloves, crushed
sea salt and freshly ground black pepper

Serves: 4 | Takes: 25 minutes

Preheat the oven to 200°C/400°F.

Spread the pasta out in a 30 x 20 x 5-cm roasting tray or dish, untangling any strands that are entwined or stuck together. Scatter over the broccoli and cheeses and toss well to combine.

Stir the sauce ingredients together with 50ml water and pour over the pasta. Using tongs, turn all the ingredients in the sauce so everything is coated; the pasta won't be submerged but that doesn't matter. Cover tightly with foil – use two layers if necessary to seal well.

Bake for 10 minutes. Remove from the oven and toss the pasta so everything gets a turn cooking in the cream. The pasta shouldn't look dry but if it does, add a splash of water. Cover tightly with the foil again and bake for a further 10 minutes. Serve immediately, with extra Parmesan on top.

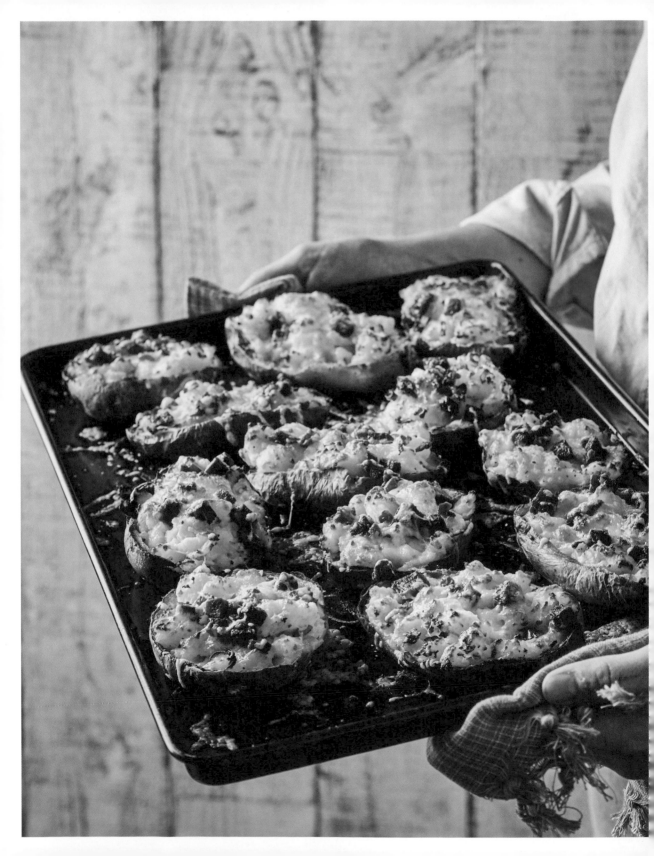

Cheesy loaded potato skins with chorizo

Sometimes the most delicious things can be the most simple, and this is one of those: soothing, tasty and filling.

6 medium baking potatoes
3 tbsp sea salt flakes
2 tbsp unsalted butter
80g cream cheese
140g grated Cheddar cheese
3 spring onions, finely sliced
sea salt and freshly ground black pepper
80g cooking chorizo, chopped small

Serves: 6
Takes: about 1 hour 40 minutes

Preheat the oven to 220°C/425°F.

Wet the potatoes, shake off any excess water and sprinkle all over with the sea salt flakes. Place in a 30 x 20 x 5-cm roasting tray and bake for 1–1 hour 15 minutes, or until completely cooked through and tender.

Brush the salt off the potatoes and cut in half lengthways. Scoop the potato flesh into a bowl being careful not to split the skins. Add the butter, cream cheese and half the Cheddar to the potatoes and mix until smoothish. Stir in the spring onions and season with salt and pepper.

Fill the skins with the potato mixture and return to the roasting tray. Top each of the filled potato halves with chorizo and sprinkle over the remaining Cheddar. Bake for a further 10–15 minutes, or until the cheese is bubbling. Serve immediately.

Dinner

Seafood, chorizo and potato stew with saffron

Pork and seafood are an ace combination and this quick dish is no exception. Salty, smoky, spicy chorizo pairs perfectly with sweet prawns, mussels and clams, which release their briny juices as they steam. A chunk of bread to mop up the broth is the only extra you need.

200g cooking chorizo, cut into
   2-cm pieces
400g new potatoes, cut into 5-mm slices
splash of olive oil
400ml fish stock (a good stock/bouillon
   cube dissolved in boiling water is fine)
4 tbsp unsalted butter
½ tsp saffron strands, chopped
2 garlic cloves, crushed
600g live mussels, rinsed
   and scrubbed
200g raw king prawns, weighed without
   heads or shells
600g clams
120ml dry white wine
sea salt and freshly ground black pepper
finely grated zest of ½ lemon
handful of chopped flat leaf parsley

Serves: 4 | Takes: about 45 minutes

Preheat the oven to 230°C/450°F.

Place the chorizo and potatoes in a 30 x 20 x 5-cm roasting tray, toss with the olive oil and roast for 20 minutes until sizzling and the potatoes are tender.

Add the stock, butter, saffron, garlic, mussels, prawns, clams and wine to the tray, season with salt and pepper and give it a little shake. Cover tightly with foil and roast for 12 minutes, or until the prawns are pink and the mussels and clams have opened (discard any unopened ones). Serve immediately, sprinkled with lemon zest and parsley.

Salmon fillets with vine tomatoes, beans and green sauce

This is one of the best ways to cook salmon fillets – they're pretty much steamed, with just a few aromatics and vegetables. The green sauce is intense and punchy; perfect with fish, it's also fantastic spooned over lamb and chicken.

250g cherry tomatoes, on the vine
  if possible
200g green beans, trimmed
2 tbsp extra virgin olive oil
sea salt and freshly ground black pepper
4 salmon fillets, about 130g each and
  about 3cm thick at thickest point
1 lemon
few dill sprigs (optional)

For the green sauce (optional):
2 tbsp capers, well rinsed
6 anchovy fillets
2 garlic cloves, crushed
20g flat leaf parsley leaves and fine stalks
20g basil leaves and fine stalks
2 shallots, roughly chopped
2 tbsp lemon juice
½ tsp Dijon mustard
120ml extra virgin olive oil,
  or more if needed

Serves: 4 | Takes: 25 minutes

Preheat the oven to 220°C/425°F.

Place the tomatoes and beans in a 30 x 20 x 5-cm roasting tray and pour over 1 tablespoon of the olive oil. Toss to coat and season generously with salt and pepper. Brush the salmon fillets on both sides with olive oil, season with salt and pepper, then add to the roasting tray with the tomatoes and beans.

Thinly slice half the lemon, and arrange the slices on the fish. Squeeze the juice from the remaining lemon half over the fish and vegetables, and tuck in the dill. Cover tightly with foil and bake for 12 minutes, or until just cooked through. If the beans need a little more time, remove the fish and tomatoes from the tray and return to the oven for a few minutes.

Meanwhile, blitz the sauce ingredients together in a food processor until not quite smooth. Have a taste and add more lemon juice or pepper if needed – it shouldn't need any salt.

Serve the salmon with the sauce and vegetables.

Lamb loin with harissa and sweet potato mash

This dish has bags of flavour and looks like you've gone to a lot of trouble to make it, when actually it's a doddle. Just make sure you buy a good-quality jar of rose harissa paste.

2 thick lamb neck fillets, about 600g in total
1 tsp sea salt flakes, plus extra for seasoning
freshly ground black pepper
2 heaped tbsp rose harissa paste
800g sweet potato, peeled and cut into 3-cm pieces
3 sage leaves or bay leaves
3 tbsp olive oil
3 garlic cloves, unpeeled
½ tsp ground cinnamon
½ tsp chilli flakes
1 tbsp unsalted butter
bitter green salad, to serve (optional)

Serves: 4 | Takes: 1 hour

Pat the lamb dry with kitchen paper and season with salt and pepper. Rub all over with the harissa paste and set aside for at least 10 minutes.

Preheat the oven to 220°C/425°F.

Place the sweet potato, sage or bay leaves, olive oil, garlic, cinnamon, chilli flakes, the 1 teaspoon of salt and 3 tablespoons of water in a 30 x 20 x 5-cm roasting tray. Toss well with your hands so everything is combined and the sweet potato is coated in spiced oil. Add the butter to the tray and roast for 25 minutes, shaking the tray occasionally.

Push the sweet potato to one side – it should still fit in a single layer – and add the lamb. Roast for 12–15 minutes, turning the lamb over and shaking the tray halfway through. When done, it should still be springy to touch. Transfer to a plate, cover loosely with foil and leave to rest for 10 minutes.

Meanwhile, remove the sage or bay leaves and squeeze the garlic out of its papery skin into the tray with the sweet potato. Mash, incorporating all the meat juices from the tray, and season with more salt and pepper if needed.

Cut the lamb into thick slices and serve with the sweet potato mash, pouring any lamb juices from the plate over the meat. This is lovely served with a bitter green salad.

Roast hake with Parmesan crust, chorizo and sweet potatoes

Have your oven lovely and hot for this one so the crust turns crisp and golden. Keep an eye on the fish – thick fillets will need a little longer than thin ones, and you don't want to overcook them.

4 thick hake fillets (cod is also fine)
2 tbsp olive oil, plus extra for brushing
sea salt and freshly ground black pepper
700g sweet potatoes, cut into
   3-cm chunks
about 60g chorizo, finely sliced
2 large handfuls of spinach
1 lemon, cut into quarters

For the crust:
60g sourdough breadcrumbs (or similar)
25g grated Parmesan cheese
1 garlic clove, crushed
handful of flat leaf parsley leaves and fine
   stalks, finely chopped
finely grated zest ½ lemon
2 tbsp olive oil

Serves: 4 | Takes: 45 minutes

Preheat the oven to 220°C/425°F.

Lightly brush both sides of the fish with olive oil and season generously with salt and pepper. Set aside.

Place the sweet potatoes in a 30 x 20 x 5-cm roasting tray, toss with the 2 tablespoons of olive oil and season generously with salt and pepper. Roast for 20 minutes, shaking the tray halfway through.

Meanwhile, toss all the ingredients for the crust together in a bowl.

When the sweet potatoes have had their 20 minutes, remove the tray from the oven and nestle the fish fillets into the tray, skin-side down if they have skin. Arrange a single layer of chorizo on top of each fillet, then cover with the crust mixture, pressing down gently to keep it in place. Roast for 10–15 minutes, or until the fish is just cooked through and the crust is golden.

Transfer the fish to warmed serving plates. Add the spinach to the roasting tray and toss with the sweet potatoes. The spinach should wilt slightly in the residual heat of the roasting tray. Serve immediately with the fish, and lemon wedges for squeezing over the fish.

Sea bass with stewed summer vegetables

Roasting the vegetables brings out their gorgeous sweetness, and almost stews them into loveliness. Please be careful not to overcook the fish – it's criminal in a dish this delicious.

4 sea bass fillets
sea salt flakes and freshly ground
    black pepper
2 red onions, finely sliced
6 tbsp extra olive oil, plus extra
    if needed
2 tbsp unsalted butter
2 red peppers, finely sliced
350g ripe tomatoes, roughly chopped
handful of black olives, halved
1 courgette, about 225g, halved
    lengthways and sliced into half-moons
2 garlic cloves, crushed
handful of flat leaf parsley, chopped
1 tbsp dried oregano
3 tbsp balsamic vinegar
crusty bread, to serve

Serves: 4 | Takes: 1 hour 15 minutes

Preheat the oven to 200°C/400°F. Pat the fish dry with kitchen paper and season generously with salt and pepper. Set aside.

Spread the onions out in a 30 x 20 x 5-cm roasting tray, toss with 3 tablespoons of the oil and season generously with salt and pepper. Roast for 10 minutes, shaking the tray halfway through.

Remove the tray from the oven and stir the butter into the onions until melted. Add all the remaining ingredients, including the remaining olive oil and more salt and pepper, but not the fish. Toss so everything is well combined.

Roast for 40 minutes, shaking the tray occasionally, until the vegetables are very tender and releasing their juices – if they look a little dry add a splash more olive oil.

Remove the tray from the oven, add the fish, skin-side up, and drizzle with olive oil. Roast for 8–10 minutes (the exact time will depend on the thickness of your fish) until just cooked through. Remove the skin from the fish and serve immediately with the vegetables spooned over, and crusty bread for dunking in the oily juices.

Veal parmigiana

This Italian classic is loved all over the world, and rightly so. Thin slices of breadcrumbed veal, layered up with tomato sauce, mozzarella and Parmesan, then baked, ticks all the boxes for a hearty, tasty feast. If you prefer, swap the veal for chicken breasts bashed thin between sheets of clingfilm.

50g golden breadcrumbs
60g grated Parmesan cheese
50g plain flour
sea salt and freshly ground black pepper
1 large egg, lightly beaten
400g high-welfare veal escalope,
    cut into 4 equal pieces
oil, for brushing
200g canned chopped tomatoes
1 garlic clove, crushed
2 tsp dried marjoram
1 tbsp olive oil
½ tsp sea salt
¼ tsp caster sugar
100g mozzarella balls, sliced
salad, to serve

Serves: 4 | Takes: 35 minutes

Preheat the oven to 220°C/425°F.

Combine the breadcrumbs and 20g of the Parmesan in a shallow bowl. Put the flour in another bowl and season with salt and pepper. Place the beaten egg in a third shallow bowl.

Pat the veal dry with kitchen paper and season generously with salt and pepper. Coat both sides of the veal with the flour, then dip in the egg, then the breadcrumbs, pressing down so they stick. Set a wire rack over a 30 x 20 x 5-cm roasting tray, lightly brush the rack with oil and place the crumbed escalopes on top. Roast for 12 minutes, or until crisp on the outside and just cooked through.

Meanwhile, combine the tomatoes, garlic, marjoram, olive oil, the ½ teaspoon of sea salt, the sugar, and some pepper in a bowl.

Reduce the oven temperature to 180°C/350°F and carefully transfer the escalopes from the rack to the roasting tray using a spatula. Cover each escalope generously with tomato sauce and top with the sliced mozzarella. Add more tomato sauce on top and sprinkle over the remaining Parmesan. Roast for 10 minutes, or until the cheese is melted and bubbling and the tomato sauce is hot. Serve immediately with salad.

Rare roast beef with hasselback potatoes and green beans

Like the chicken recipe on page 126, this is a complete roast meal for four people cooked in just one vessel: huzzah for minimal washing up! The hasselback potatoes take a tad more effort than standard roasties, but they're worth it, as they soak up all the delicious juices from the beef.

1.5kg boned joint of beef (topside/round or sirloin)
1 tbsp mustard powder or finely ground mustard seeds
sea salt and freshly ground black pepper
3 tbsp dripping or lard
8 medium potatoes
250g fine green beans, trimmed
splash of olive oil
squeeze of lemon juice

Serves: 4 | Takes: about 1 hour 20 minutes

Preheat the oven to 240°C/475°F.

Pat the beef dry with kitchen paper, and rub all over with the mustard and salt and pepper. Place in a 30 x 20 x 5-cm roasting tray, add the fat or lard and roast for 15 minutes, basting halfway through.

Meanwhile, peel the potatoes, then cut slits a few millimetres apart almost to the bottom, so the slices stay connected. The easiest way to do this is to sit a potato in the hollow of a wooden spoon – the edges of the spoon will prevent the knife from slicing all the way through.

Reduce the oven temperature to 180°C/350°F. Add the potatoes to the tray, spoon over lots of the hot fat and season generously with salt and pepper. Roast for 40 minutes, basting the beef and potatoes frequently – for medium-rare or medium roast for 5–10 minutes longer.

Meanwhile, toss the beans in the olive oil and some lemon juice and season with salt and pepper.

Remove the beef from the roasting tray and transfer to a plate. Cover loosely with foil and set aside. Nudge the potatoes to one side of the roasting tray, add the beans (spread them out as much as possible) and return to the oven. Increase the oven temperature to 200°C/400°F and roast for 15 minutes, shaking the tray occasionally.

Carve the beef into thick slices and serve with the potatoes and beans, with the rested meat juices poured over.

Pork sausages with fennel, apples and red wine gravy

Apple is a perfect foil for the fatty sausages and rich wine gravy, and served with some green leaves, this makes a complete meal. Obviously it also goes beautifully with creamy mashed potato, so if you have some to hand then all the better.

8 large good-quality pork sausages
2 tbsp olive oil
1 large fennel bulb, trimmed, halved and thickly sliced (fronds reserved)
2 medium eating apples
sea salt and freshly ground black pepper
300ml light red wine
50ml chicken or vegetable stock
1½ tbsp balsamic vinegar
3 tbsp unsalted butter
1 tsp fennel seeds, crushed

Serves: 4 | Takes: 1 hour 15 minutes

Preheat the oven to 220°C/425°F.

Place the sausages in a 30 x 20 x 5-cm roasting tray, toss with 1 tablespoon of the olive oil and roast for 20 minutes, shaking the tray halfway through. They should take on some lovely colour.

Reduce the oven temperature to 180°C/350°F and add the sliced fennel to the tray. Core and quarter the apples, then cut into thick slices – there's no need to peel them – and add to the tray, too. Toss with the remaining oil – the tray will be crowded but that's fine, as everything will cook down a little. Season with salt and pepper and roast for a further 30 minutes.

Add the wine, stock, balsamic vinegar, butter and fennel seeds to the tray, season with salt and pepper and shake well. Roast for a further 15 minutes, or until the red wine has reduced a little and the gravy is bubbling nicely. Serve immediately, garnished with the reserved fennel fronds.

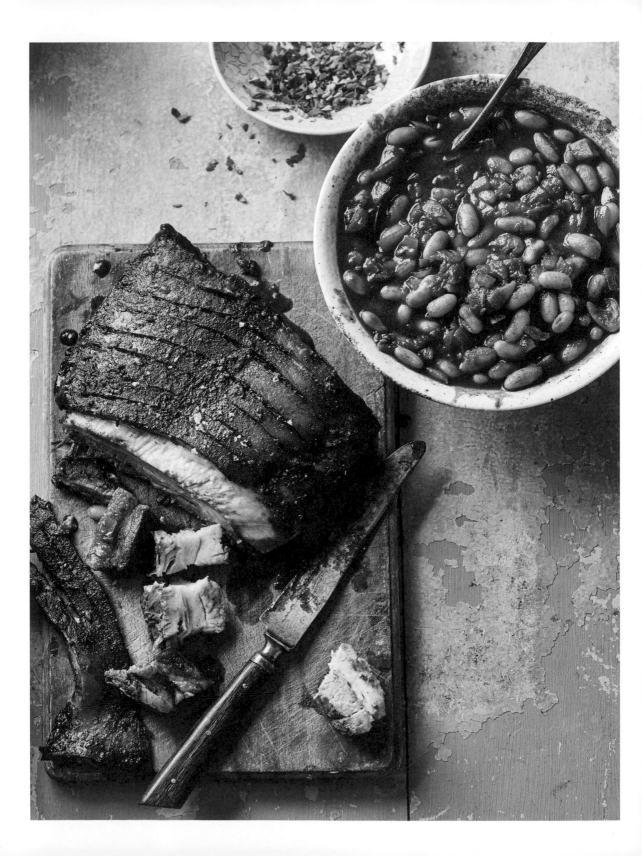

Pork belly with smoky beans

Pork belly is still a relatively inexpensive cut of meat that's soft and tender when cooked low and slow. Here the porky flavours melt into the beans to produce a dish that's insanely comforting and delicious. It does take a few hours to cook, but almost all of this is hands-off time in the oven.

1.5kg pork belly
2 x 400-g cans cannellini or butter
   beans, drained
chopped flat leaf parsley, to serve

For the sauce:
1 onion, finely chopped
400g canned chopped tomatoes
2 garlic cloves, crushed
2 tbsp tomato purée
5 tbsp apple cider vinegar
1 tbsp treacle
2 tbsp smoked paprika
2 tsp English mustard powder
2 tsp chilli powder
1 tsp fennel seeds
1 tsp ground cinnamon
3 tsp sea salt

Serves: 4 | Takes: 3 hours 15 minutes

Preheat the oven to 160°C/325°F.

Place all the sauce ingredients, including 800ml just-boiled water, in a 30 x 20 x 5 cm roasting tray and mix well. Place the pork belly on top, skin-side up. Spoon some of the liquid over the pork and rub into the skin. Cover loosely with foil and roast for 1½ hours.

Remove the foil, baste the pork with the sauce and roast, uncovered, for a further hour, adding water to the tray as needed to prevent the sauce drying out.

Stir the beans into the sauce, adding more water if too thick, and roast for a final 30 minutes. The beans should be cooking in a thick rich sauce.

When done, remove the skin from the pork, cut the meat into pieces and stir into the beans and sauce. Serve immediately, with chopped parsley.

Celeriac, potato and anchovy gratin

Knobbly old celeriac is a sadly undervalued root vegetable. It might not be photogenic, but it's absolutely delicious, with a sweet, nutty flavour reminiscent of the celery family of which it is a member. The anchovies add a gorgeous depth of flavour – no fishiness at all.

400ml milk, plus extra if needed
400ml double cream
2 garlic cloves, crushed
3 anchovy fillets, very finely chopped
2–3 thyme sprigs
freshly ground black pepper
300g celeriac
300g waxy potatoes
100g grated Comté cheese
green salad, to serve (optional)

For the topping:
100g sourdough or country-style
    bread, torn into small pieces
2 tbsp olive oil
30g grated Parmesan cheese

Serves: 4 | Takes: about 1 hour,
    plus 5 minutes cooling

Preheat the oven to 190°C/375°F. Combine the milk, cream, garlic, anchovies and thyme in a 30 x 20 x 5-cm roasting tray and season with pepper.

Peel and very finely slice the celeriac and potatoes, ideally on a mandoline, adding the vegetables to the creamy tray liquid as you go to prevent them browning. Bake for 20 minutes, shaking the tray halfway through. Add a little more milk if necessary so the vegetables are just submerged.

Meanwhile, mix all the topping ingredients together in a bowl. Set aside.

When the vegetables have had their 20 minutes, sprinkle over the Comté, then the topping mix. Bake for a further 30 minutes – the vegetables should be beautifully tender when the time is up. Leave to cool in the tray for 5 minutes before serving – a green salad is the perfect accompaniment.

Spiced vegetables and chickpeas with yoghurt and mint

Curry powder sometimes raises eyebrows among purists but there's nothing wrong with a shortcut now and then, as long as you layer other flavours into the dish. Seek out a good-quality hot curry powder and you won't look back.

6 tbsp rapeseed oil or other flavourless oil, plus extra if needed
1 medium aubergine, about 300g
½ tsp fine sea salt
2 medium onions, roughly chopped
300g cauliflower florets, cut small
sea salt and freshly ground black pepper
4 garlic cloves, crushed
1 heaped tsp grated fresh ginger
2–3 tbsp good-quality hot curry powder
2 x 400-g cans chopped tomatoes
400-g can chickpeas (not drained)
2 tsp sea salt flakes

To serve:
squeeze of lemon juice
250g Greek yoghurt
large handful of chopped mint

Serves: 4 generously | Takes: 1 hour 20 minutes, includes 20 minutes draining

Preheat the oven to 220°C/425°F. Pour the oil into a 30 x 20 x 5-cm roasting tray and place inside the oven to heat.

Meanwhile, chop the aubergine into 2-cm cubes, place in a colander and toss with the ½ teaspoon of salt. Set the colander over a bowl or sink to drain for 20 minutes. Spread the aubergine out on kitchen paper, pat dry and squeeze out any excess moisture.

Carefully place the onions, aubergine and cauliflower into the hot oil in the roasting tray, season with salt and pepper and toss to coat. Roast for 20–25 minutes, shaking the tray occasionally, or until the vegetables are almost tender and a little browned at the edges.

Add the garlic, ginger and curry powder to the tray and mix in well, adding a little more oil to moisten the spices if too dry. Return the tray to the oven for 5 minutes.

Add the chopped tomatoes, the chickpeas with the can water, and the sea salt flakes to the tray and stir. Return to the oven for 30 minutes, stirring once or twice, or until the sauce is bubbling and slightly reduced, and the vegetables and chickpeas are very tender.

Serve with a squeeze of lemon, a spoonful of yoghurt on top and a generous sprinkling of mint.

Chicken thighs with creamy leek and caper sauce

The sauce here is a gorgeous one, with the rich and creamy notes lifted by the sharp saltiness of the capers. It really does make you wonder why anything is cooked on the stove.

8 chicken thighs, skin on
450g new potatoes, halved
   (or quartered if large)
2 tbsp olive oil
sea salt and freshly ground black pepper
180ml double cream
100ml dry vermouth (Noilly Prat is
   great) or white wine
1 tsp bouillon powder
2 garlic cloves, crushed
1 large leek, finely sliced
30g capers
2 handfuls of watercress

Serves: 4–6 | Takes: about 1 hour

Preheat the oven to 220°C/425°F.

Place the chicken and potatoes in a 30 x 20 x 5-cm roasting tray and toss with the olive oil. Arrange the chicken skin-side up and season generously with salt and pepper. Roast for 25 minutes until the skin is crisp and starting to turn golden.

Meanwhile, combine all the remaining ingredients, except the watercress, with 100ml boiling water in a jug, then season with salt and pepper. When the cooking time for the chicken and potatoes is up, pour the creamy mixture into the tray, then turn the chicken in the liquid to coat but return the chicken to skin-side up.

Roast for a further 30 minutes until the chicken is cooked through and the sauce is bubbling. Serve with the watercress scattered on top.

Oven 'fried' buttermilk chicken with corn and greens

The highlight of this Southern-inspired feast is the chicken: it's ridiculously tender, juicy and tasty thanks to its lengthy bath in a buttermilk marinade. It really does make all the difference.

8 chicken drumsticks, skin removed
50g panko breadcrumbs
4 tbsp golden breadcrumbs
1 tsp paprika
1 tsp cayenne pepper
½ tsp fine sea salt
1 tsp garlic powder
olive oil, for drizzling and brushing
4 small corn on the cobs, or 2 cobs cut in half
2 tbsp unsalted butter
½ tsp smoked paprika
sea salt and freshly ground black pepper
160g spring greens, sliced

For the marinade:
2 tbsp lemon juice
250ml buttermilk or plain yoghurt
2 garlic cloves, crushed
2 tsp Dijon mustard
½ tsp dried oregano
½ tsp sea salt
¼ tsp freshly ground black pepper

Serves: 4 | Takes: 55 minutes, plus at least 2 hours marinating

Mix all the marinade ingredients together in a large zip-lock bag. Add the chicken and squelch the contents to ensure the chicken is completely coated in the marinade. Chill in the fridge for at least 2 hours, or ideally overnight. Remove from the fridge 30 minutes before cooking.

Preheat the oven to 200°C/400°F.

Mix both breadcrumbs, the paprika, cayenne, salt and garlic powder together in a shallow bowl. Shake any excess marinade off the chicken and dredge in the breadcrumb mixture, pressing down to ensure the coating sticks. Transfer to a lightly oiled wire rack as you go.

Spread each of the cobs with one-quarter of the butter and sprinkle with a pinch of smoked paprika and salt and pepper. Wrap tightly in foil. Place in a 30 x 20 x 5-cm roasting tray. Sit the rack bearing the chicken over the tray and transfer to the oven. Roast for about 35 minutes until the chicken is cooked through and the coating is crisp.

Meanwhile, toss the greens with a splash of olive oil and season with salt and pepper. Five minutes before the chicken has finished cooking, push the corn to one side and add the greens to the roasting tray. Push the chicken to one side so that it sits over the corn, not the greens (the steam tends to make the coating go soggy) and cook for the final 5 minutes. Serve immediately.

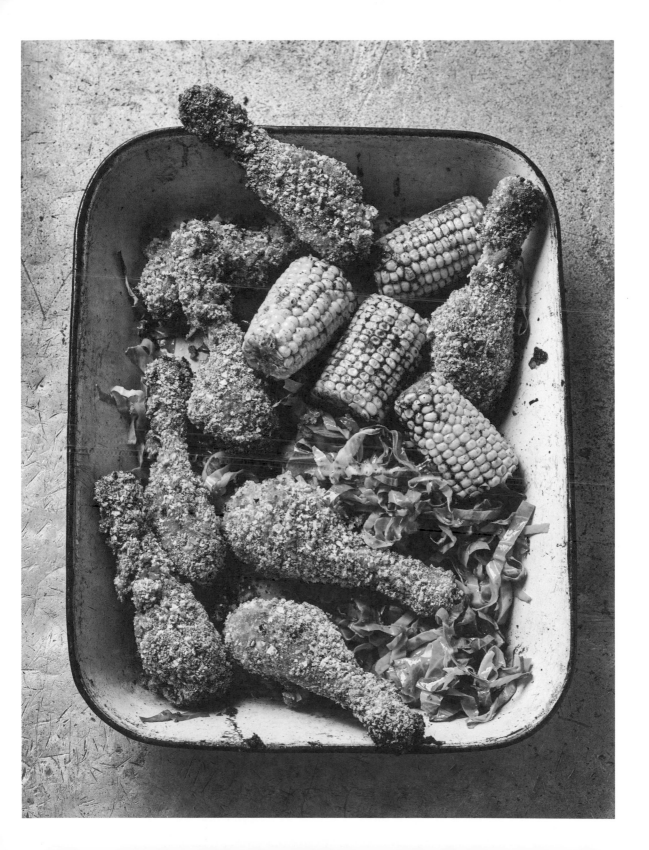

Duck breasts with juniper, blackberry and port sauce

Dark, rich and a little gamey, duck breast is gorgeous paired with blackberries in a mellow port sauce. The skin does not turn quite as crisp as it does when cooked the conventional way, seared first in a frying pan on the stove, but it is delicious nonetheless.

2 boneless duck breasts, skin on
10 juniper berries, crushed
½ tsp sea salt flakes
3 garlic cloves, unpeeled and bashed
small bunch of thyme
salad or greens, to serve (optional)

For the sauce:
5 tbsp port
180ml beef stock
25g light brown soft sugar
2 tbsp unsalted butter
150g blackberries

Serves: 2 | Takes: 35–40 minutes

Preheat the oven to 240°C/475°F and place a 30 x 20 x 5-cm roasting tray inside on the highest rack to heat.

Pat the duck dry with kitchen paper and score the skin diagonally with a sharp knife. Using a pestle, bash the juniper berries with the salt in a mortar, then rub the mixture into the duck skin.

When the oven has reached the correct temperature, quickly place the duck breasts, skin-side down, in the hot tray and roast for 5 minutes.

Reduce the oven temperature to 200°C/400°F, turn the duck breasts over and baste with the rendered fat. Add the garlic and thyme to the tray, shake well and roast for a further 10 minutes, basting halfway through.

Transfer the duck to a plate and cover loosely with foil. Tip out all but 2 tablespoons of the fat from the tray. Stir in the port, stock, sugar and butter. Add the blackberries and squash them a bit with a fork. Return to the oven for 12 minutes – the mixture should thicken slightly.

Remove and discard the thyme sprigs. Squeeze out the garlic flesh and discard the skins. Mash the berries and garlic with a fork and amalgamate into the sauce, adding in any juices from the duck plate.

Serve the duck in slices with the sauce spooned over. Some new potatoes and salad or greens would be lovely alongside.

Risotto with smoked mackerel, peas and lemon

Smoked mackerel is a rich and incredibly tasty oily fish, and it's widely available, which really makes this dish a winner.

1 tbsp olive oil
2 tbsp unsalted butter
1 small onion, grated
1 fat garlic clove, crushed
300g risotto rice
800ml fish stock/broth (good-quality stock cube or bouillon is fine), plus a splash extra if needed
50ml dry sherry (dry vermouth or white wine also works well)
1 tsp hot smoked paprika
½ tsp sea salt
2 smoked mackerel fillets, skin removed and flaked
70g frozen peas
3 tbsp crème fraîche
finely grated zest of ½ lemon and lemon juice, to taste
2 tbsp chopped dill

Serves: 2–4 | Takes: 30 minutes

Preheat the oven to 200°C/400°F.

Place the olive oil and butter in a 30 x 20 x 5-cm roasting tray and transfer to the oven for 2–3 minutes to melt. Add the onion and garlic, toss well to coat in the oil and bake for 5 minutes to soften.

Add the rice to the tray, stir to coat in the buttery oil, then add the stock, sherry, paprika and salt. Cover tightly with foil and bake for 15 minutes.

Stir in the mackerel, peas and crème fraîche. Add a splash more stock if the rice is looking a little dry, recover with foil and bake for a further 5 minutes. Stir in the lemon zest and juice (to taste) and dill and serve immediately.

Beef and chilli meatballs

It is a truth universally acknowledged that you can never have too many meatballs, so this recipe makes enough for six hungry meatball-lovers. Alternatively, they make fantastic canapés – just transfer to a platter with the sauce, spear the balls with toothpicks and pass around.

extra virgin olive oil, for brushing
1kg beef mince
1 tbsp chilli flakes
1 tbsp smoked paprika
1 tbsp nigella seeds
2 tsp ground cumin
2 garlic cloves, crushed
2 large eggs, lightly beaten
50g soft breadcrumbs
80g grated Parmesan cheese
sea salt flakes and freshly ground
    black pepper
750g passata
½ tsp caster sugar

Makes: 40 balls | Takes 45 minutes

Preheat the oven to 220°C/425°F and brush a 30 x 20 x 5-cm roasting tray with olive oil.

Place all the ingredients, except half the Parmesan, all the passata and sugar, in a mixing bowl. Mix well with your hands until everything is beautifully combined. Season well with salt and pepper.

Using damp hands, roll the mixture into golf ball-sized balls (roughly 30g each) and transfer to the prepared roasting tray. They will be quite snug, so place them close together. Brush with olive oil and roast for 20 minutes.

Mix the passata and sugar together, then pour over the meatballs and season well with salt and pepper. Sprinkle over the remaining Parmesan.

Bake for a further 15 minutes until the sauce is bubbling and the meatballs are cooked through. Serve immediately.

Roast chicken dinner with apple and pistachio stuffing

Fact: there is no easier way to cook a roast chicken dinner with all the trimmings than this. Roasting the bird directly on the oven rack allows all the delicious chicken juices to fall through to the vegetables below. And there are even greens and gravy.

1 medium free-range chicken, about 1.5kg
rapeseed oil, for drizzling
sea salt and freshly ground black pepper
300g small carrots
700g potatoes, ideally Maris Piper or Yukon Gold
150g cavolo nero, tough stems removed and finely sliced
200ml hot chicken stock

For the stuffing:
1 medium apple, peeled, cored and diced very small
80g breadcrumbs, ideally from a sourdough or good-quality, country-style loaf
40g pistachio nuts, roughly chopped
1 large egg, lightly beaten
2 garlic cloves, crushed
1 tsp fennel seeds, crushed in a mortar
grated zest ½ lemon

Serves: 4 | Time: 1 hour 30 minutes

Preheat the oven to 240°C/475°F. Set the oven rack on the middle shelf and another underneath, leaving just enough space between to fit a 30 x 20 x 5-cm roasting tray.

Mix all the stuffing ingredients together and stuff into the chicken's cavity. Pat the chicken dry with kitchen paper. Drizzle over some oil, sprinkle generously with salt and pepper, then rub into the skin. Place the bird on the top rack and slot the oven tray on the shelf underneath so it can catch the fat from the bird. Roast for 15 minutes.

Meanwhile, cut any carrots bigger than the width of your thumb in half or quarters lengthways. Peel the potatoes and cut into quarters, or eighths if very large, ideally no larger than 5cm wide. When the chicken has had its 15 minutes, reduce the oven temperature to 200°C/400°F. Add the vegetables to the tray and turn them in the hot fat; add a little more oil if necessary to lightly coat, and season generously with salt and pepper. Place the tray directly underneath the chicken again and roast for 50 minutes, shaking the tray occasionally.

Add the cavolo nero to the tray, pour over half the stock and gently turn the vegetables so the kale is coated in the liquid and sitting among the potatoes and carrots, not on top. Roast for 10 minutes.

Transfer the chicken and vegetables to serving plates. Pour the remaining stock into the tray, stir to incorporate the juices and caramelised bits to make a light gravy. Spoon over the chicken and vegetables and serve immediately.

Saffron rice with chicken, seafood and sherry

Purists would have a field day if this dish were ever called paella – so let's not speak of it. Suffice to say this is 'inspired' by that classic dish and uses lots of Spanish flavours to produce a hearty and deeply flavourful rice feast.

4 chicken thighs, skin on
olive oil, for drizzling
sea salt and freshly ground black pepper
1 large red onion, chopped
1 red pepper, deseeded and chopped
3 garlic cloves, crushed
1l chicken stock
2 tbsp dry sherry
2 ripe tomatoes, peeled and diced
1 tbsp smoked paprika
1 bay leaf
pinch of saffron strands, finely chopped
400g paella rice
80g frozen peas
8 raw king prawns, peeled and heads removed (optional)
100g squid rings
lemon wedges, to serve

Serves: 4 | Takes: 1 hour 10 minutes

Preheat the oven to 200°C/400°F.

Place the chicken in a 30 x 20 x 5-cm roasting tray, skin-side up, drizzle over a little olive oil and season with salt and pepper. Roast for 25 minutes until the skin is golden. Remove from the tray and set aside.

Discard all but 2 tablespoons of fat from the tray. Add the onion, pepper and garlic, toss to coat and roast for 10 minutes until softened.

Pour in the stock and stir to scrape up any caramelised bits on the bottom. Add the sherry, tomatoes, paprika, bay leaf, saffron, rice and lots of salt and pepper. Stir well, then return the chicken to the tray. Cover tightly with foil and bake for 25 minutes, by which time the chicken should be cooked through.

Add the peas, prawns and squid to the tray, poking them into the rice. There should still be some liquid left to be absorbed, but if not add a splash more stock or water. Cover with foil and roast for a final 5 minutes – the prawns should be pink and the squid tender and cooked through. Serve immediately with lemon wedges.

Sweet Things

Roast apricots with cardamom, spiced cream and amaretti

This simple dessert is packed with flavour: apricots dripping with cardamom-infused honey, spiced cream and crunchy amaretti biscuits. You could make it all in advance and just assemble when needed.

12 ripe apricots, halved and pitted
4 long strips unwaxed lemon peel
12 green cardamom pods, crushed and seeds removed
6 tbsp runny honey
500ml double cream
1 heaped tbsp icing sugar, sifted
1 tsp ground cinnamon
4 amaretti biscuits, crushed

Serves: 4 | Takes: 30 minutes, plus cooling

Preheat the oven to 190°C/375°F.

Place the apricots, cut-side up, in a single layer in a 30 x 20 x 5-cm roasting tray and tuck the lemon peel between them.

Using a mortar and pestle, finely grind the cardamom seeds. Mix the cardamom together with the honey and 120ml warm water. Pour the mixture over the apricots, making sure to fill indentations in the fruit. Bake for about 20 minutes, basting occasionally. The fruit should be very tender but still holding its shape. Leave to cool to room temperature.

Very lightly whip the cream – it should flop off the spoon readily – and fold in the icing sugar and cinnamon.

To assemble, layer the apricots and cream into four serving glasses and top with the crushed biscuits, or simply arrange on plates. Serve immediately.

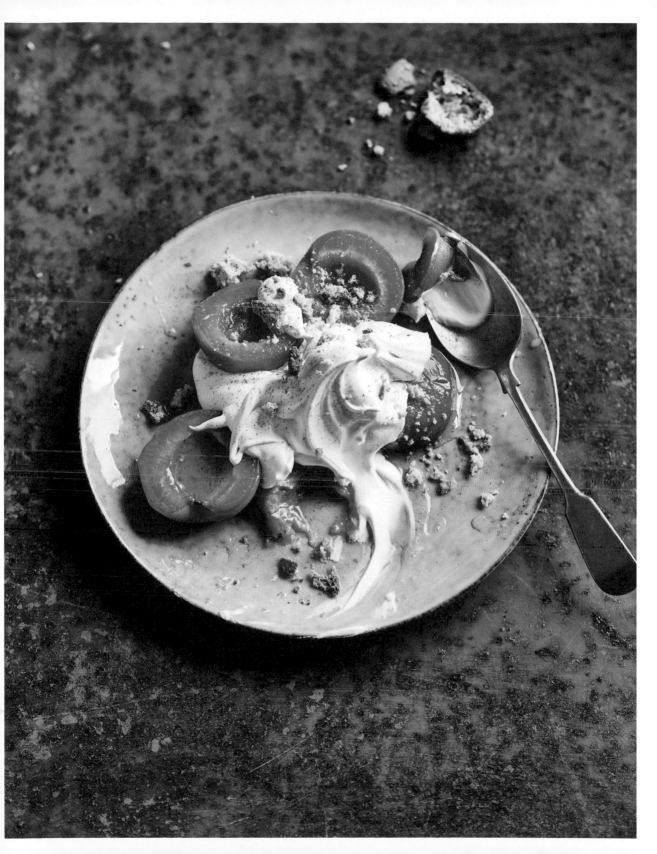

Peanut butter caramel brownies

These are very rich and chocolatey, their sweetness tempered by the lovely savoury note of peanuts – basically, they're the ultimate roasting tray treat.

vegetable oil, or other flavourless oil, for brushing
350g caramel sauce, from a can or jar
80g smooth or crunchy peanut butter, ideally no added sugar
120g plain flour
75g unsweetened cocoa powder
generous pinch of salt
½ tsp baking powder
230g unsalted butter, softened
300g golden caster sugar
3 large eggs
1 tsp vanilla extract
200g dark chocolate chips

Makes: 12 generous squares
Takes: 1 hour

Preheat the oven to 180°C/350°F. Line a 30 x 20 x 5-cm roasting tray with baking parchment, letting it overhang the sides, and lightly brush with oil.

Stir the caramel and peanut butter together to make a smooth, pouring consistency. Set aside.

Whisk the flour, cocoa powder, salt and baking powder together in a bowl.

Beat the butter and sugar together with electric beaters or an electric mixer until fluffy. Gradually beat in the eggs, then the vanilla extract. Stir in the flour mixture to make a very thick batter, then fold in the chocolate chips.

Add half the peanut butter caramel to the batter and semi-mix it in – you want to retain some visible swirls. Spread out evenly in the prepared tray, then pour the remaining peanut butter caramel on top.

Bake for about 25 minutes, or until firm to touch. The caramel itself might be a bit gooey but will firm up as it cools. Leave in the tray for 10 minutes then use the foil to lift the brownies out onto a chopping board. When cool, cut into 12 large squares.

Polenta slices with blackberries and apple

This is a slab of gorgeousness: tender chunks of apple in a buttery, lemony cake and studded with juicy berries. It can make a lovely pudding served with lightly whipped cream. Or pack it for a picnic.

250g unsalted butter, softened,
   plus extra for greasing
160g ground almonds
160g fine polenta or semolina/cornmeal
   (it must be finely ground)
160g self-raising flour
2 tsp baking powder
pinch of salt
250g golden caster sugar
4 large eggs, lightly beaten
finely grated zest and juice of 2 lemons
350g eating apples
3 tbsp milk
150g blackberries

Makes: 12 large slices
Takes: 50 minutes

Preheat the oven to 180°C/350°F. Line a 30 x 20 x 5-cm roasting tray with foil so that it overhangs the sides. You will probably need to use two sheets, one lengthways and one crossways. Butter the foil well.

Whisk the almonds, polenta or semolina, flour, baking powder and salt together in a bowl and set aside. Beat the butter and sugar together in another bowl, ideally with electric beater until light and fluffy. Slowly beat in the eggs and lemon zest.

Peel, core and chop the apples into 5-mm cubes, transferring to a bowl and tossing with a little of the lemon juice as you go to prevent them discolouring.

Gradually stir the flour mixture into the eggs and butter mixture, alternating with the lemon juice and milk, to make a smooth batter. Fold in the apples.

Scrape the mixture into the prepared tray and smooth the top with a spatula. Press the blackberries into the top, pushing them down well.

Bake for 30 minutes until a skewer pushed into the centre comes out clean. Cool in the tray, then cut into 12 large squares.

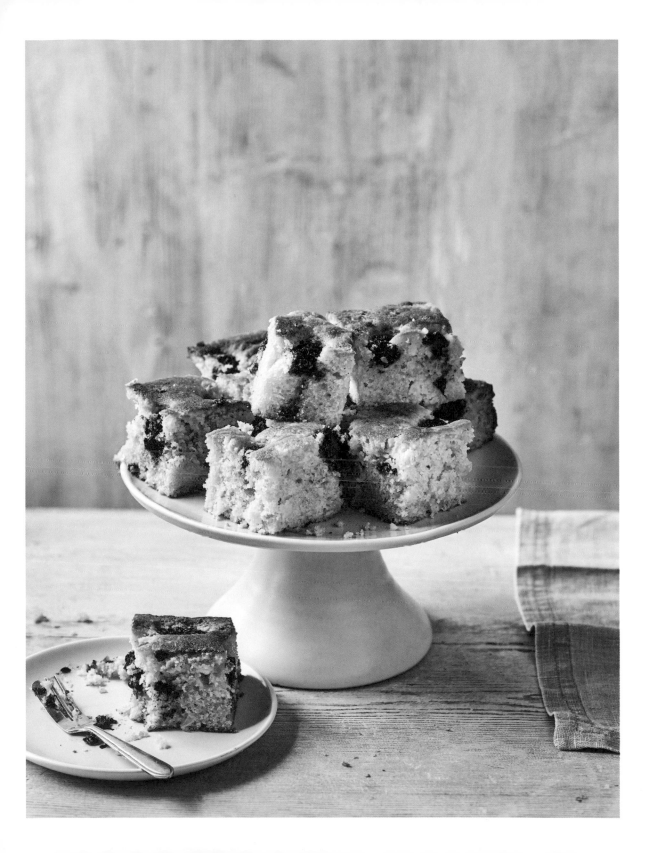

Raspberry jam tart biscuits

These are an addictive cross between a tart and a biscuit – hence the name. But whatever you call them, the tender, buttery pastry filled with toasted hazelnuts and slicked with raspberry jam is quite irresistible.

125g blanched hazelnuts
225g unsalted butter, plus extra for the
    tray if needed
280g plain flour, plus extra for dusting
1 tsp mixed spice
½ tsp fine sea salt
180g caster sugar
1 large egg
1 vanilla pod, split in half lengthways
    and seeds scraped out
225g raspberry jam, at room temperature

Makes: 12 | Takes: 1 hour

Preheat the oven to 180°C/350°F.

Place the hazelnuts in a 30 x 20 x 5-cm roasting tray. Roast for up to 10 minutes, or until golden, shaking the tray halfway through – keep an eye on them so they don't burn. Cool for a few minutes, then blitz in a food processor until finely ground. Set side to cool completely.

Meanwhile, line the roasting tray with baking parchment so it overhangs the sides; a few dabs of butter in the tray will help to keep it in place, if needed. Tip the cooled nuts into a mixing bowl, add the flour, mixed spice and salt and whisk together. Set aside.

Beat the butter and sugar together with electric beaters or an electric mixer until fluffy, then beat in the egg and vanilla seeds. Gradually stir the flour mixture into the butter mixture to make a soft dough. Set aside about 350g, or roughly one-third, of the mixture for the topping, and spoon the rest into the prepared roasting tray in mounds. Using lightly floured hands, firmly press the mounds into an even layer of dough covering the base of the tray.

Stir the jam to loosen, then spread over the dough with the back of a spoon. Scatter clumps of the remaining dough on top and flatten with the back of a lightly floured spoon. There should be jam visible through gaps in the topping.

Bake for 30 minutes, or until pale gold on top. Leave to cool in the tray for 10 minutes, then carefully lift out using the baking parchment for handles. Transfer to a wire rack to cool completely, then cut into 12 rectangles.

Peach and plum pie with vanilla and almonds

In some places this kind of pie is known as a slab pie. This might reflect the way it looks, which admittedly isn't fancy. Let's call it a relaxed pie instead. Or rustic. Whatever, it's delicious.

2 sheets of ready-rolled shortcrust
   pastry, about 35 x 23cm each
800g mixed peaches and plums,
   ripe but firm
60g caster sugar
1 tbsp cornflour
1 vanilla pod, split in half lengthways
   and seeds scraped out
3 tbsp ground almonds
1 large egg, lightly beaten
2 tsp Demerara sugar
pouring cream or ice cream, to serve

Serves: 6–8 | Takes: 1 hour 10 minutes

Preheat the oven to 180°C/350°F. Line a 30 x 20 x 5-cm roasting tray with baking parchment so it overhangs the sides. Place one of the pastry sheets in the tray – it will be too big, but arrange it so the excess comes up the sides. Chill in the fridge until needed.

Halve, stone and thinly slice the peaches and plums, leaving the skin on. Place in a mixing bowl, add the sugar, cornflour and vanilla seeds and stir to combine. Set aside for 5 minutes, then stir again – the fruit should be coated in thick sugary juices.

Meanwhile, trim the second pastry sheet to a 20 x 30-cm rectangle.

Sprinkle the ground almonds over the pastry base in the roasting tray, leaving a 2-cm border. Arrange the fruit on top. Place the trimmed pastry sheet over the fruit and brush the edges with beaten egg. Fold the edges of the bottom pastry sheet up and over the top pastry sheet and press together to seal. You should have a shallow rectangular pastry package. Make several slits in the top to let out the steam, brush with egg and sprinkle with Demerara sugar.

Bake for 40–45 minutes until burnished on top and golden underneath. Serve with pouring cream or ice cream.

(Pictured overleaf)

Orange and caraway slices with orange blossom glaze

This cake is basic in a way, but the combination of orange and caraway is slightly unusual and the flavour is amazing. The simple orange glaze on top is all it needs.

200g unsalted butter, softened,
    plus extra for greasing
160g plain flour
80g spelt flour
1 tsp baking powder
generous pinch of fine sea salt
180g light brown soft sugar
3 large eggs, lightly beaten
finely grated zest and juice of 2 oranges
2 tsp caraway seeds, pounded in a mortar
    or ground in a spice grinder

For the glaze:
150g icing sugar, sifted
splash of orange blossom water or
    orange juice
finely grated zest of 1 orange
40ml milk

Makes: 12 slices | Takes: 45 minutes

Preheat the oven to 180°C/350°F. Butter a 30 x 20 x 5-cm roasting tray and line with baking parchment.

Combine the flours, baking powder and salt together in a bowl.

Beat the butter and sugar together with electric beaters or an electric mixer until fluffy. Gradually beat in the eggs, then the orange zest and caraway seeds.

Stir the butter mixture into the flour mixture, alternating with the orange juice, to make a thickish batter. Scrape into the prepared roasting tray, making it as level as you can, and smooth the top with a spatula. Bake for 20 minutes, or until firm to the touch. Leave in the tray for 5 minutes, then turn out on a wire rack to cool.

Meanwhile, combine all the glaze ingredients in a small bowl. When the cake is completely cold, spread the glaze over the top, leave to set and cut into 12 portions.

Strawberry and rhubarb brioche pudding

This is old-fashioned bread and butter pudding really, made posh with brioche and a secret layer of baked fruit. Lush.

unsalted butter for greasing
200g strawberries, hulled and halved
300g rhubarb, cut into 3-cm pieces
90g caster sugar
1 tbsp cornflour
4 large eggs
400ml double cream
400ml milk
1 vanilla pod, split in half lengthways
   and seeds scraped out
grated zest of 1 orange
1 large brioche loaf, cut into
   1-cm slices

Serves: 8 | Takes: 1 hour 20 minutes

Preheat the oven to 170°C/325°F and lightly butter a 30 x 20 x 5-cm roasting tray or dish.

Place the strawberries and rhubarb in the prepared tray, sprinkle over 40g of the sugar and the cornflour and toss to coat.

Mix the eggs, cream, milk, the remaining sugar, the vanilla seeds and orange zest together in a jug.

Working one slice at a time, dip the brioche into the cream mixture until thoroughly soaked and arrange on top of the fruit, slightly overlapping. Pour any of the remaining mixture over the top, and set aside for 15 minutes while the bread soaks.

Bake for 40–45 minutes, or until puffed and golden.

Rye gingerbread cake

Intensely gingery and fragrant, this cake is equally nice served with a cup of tea as it is eaten warm from the oven with a scoop of vanilla ice cream for dessert. The rye flour adds an extra flavour note to the scale, but it's fine to substitute with plain flour if you don't have any to hand.

200g plain flour
50g rye flour
½ tsp ground cinnamon
1 tsp ground ginger
1 tsp bicarbonate of soda
¼ tsp fine sea salt
120g unsalted butter, cut into
   very small pieces
180g golden syrup
180g black treacle
6 tbsp syrup from a jar of stem ginger
1 large egg, lightly beaten
100g chopped stem ginger from a jar

Serves: 12 | Takes: 35 minutes

Preheat the oven to 180°C/350°F. Line a 30 x 20 x 5-cm roasting tray with baking parchment – you want it to come up and over the sides, so lightly butter the tray first to keep the paper in place.

Whisk the flours, spices, bicarbonate of soda and salt together in a mixing bowl.

Place the butter in a separate bowl or jug, add 100ml just-boiled water and stir until melted. Add the golden syrup, treacle and ginger syrup, then stir in the egg.

Whisk the wet ingredients into the dry to make a smooth batter, then fold in the chopped stem ginger. Pour into the prepared roasting tray, making sure the batter is evenly spread out.

Bake for about 20 minutes, or until firm to the touch and an inserted skewer comes out clean. Leave in the roasting tray for a few minutes, then lift out onto a wire rack to cool using the overhanging baking parchment as handles.

Baked apple dumplings with blueberry and fennel seed crumble

Baked apples are gorgeous, but stuffed with fruity crumble and wrapped in a blanket of puff pastry, they're even better. This dish is extremely simple and definitely looks fancier than it is trouble to make.

2 x sheets of ready-rolled puff pastry, about 320g each
plain flour, for dusting
4 Braeburn, Granny Smith or other eating apples, about 8cm in diameter
1 large egg, lightly beaten
1 tbsp Demerara sugar, for sprinkling
cream or vanilla ice cream, to serve

For the filling:
4 tbsp rolled oats
30g dried blueberries (any other dried fruit is fine, chopped if large)
40g unsalted butter, softened
generous pinch of fine sea salt
2 tbsp maple syrup, plus extra to serve (optional)
20g toasted hazelnuts, chopped
1 tsp fennel seeds

Serves: 4 | Takes: 1 hour

Preheat the oven to 200°C/400°F and line a 30 x 20 x 5-cm roasting tray with baking parchment.

Roll out the pastry sheets on a lightly floured work surface so they are a little thinner than they come in the packet. Using a plate as a guide, cut out two 20-cm discs from each pastry sheet. Chill in the fridge until needed.

Mix all the filling ingredients together in a bowl.

Peel the apples, then remove most of the core with a small knife or apple corer. Don't cut through to the bottom – you want to leave a little apple so the filling doesn't fall through. Use a teaspoon or melon baller to widen the hole. Tightly pack the apples with the filling – it doesn't matter if some of the filling pokes over the top.

Sit one of the apples on a pastry disc and lightly moisten around the edge with water. Gather the pastry up over the apple, pleating it as you go. Pinch the pastry at the top to seal, then trim off any excess. Repeat with the remaining apples and pastry, transferring each one to the prepared roasting tray as you go.

Brush the pastry with the beaten egg and sprinkle with the Demerara sugar. Bake for 40–50 minutes, or until the pastry is puffed and golden and the apples are cooked through; an inserted skewer should go through easily. Serve hot, with cream or vanilla ice cream, drizzled with extra maple syrup, if you like.

Magic mocha pudding

This is wickedly good: an airy chocolate sponge atop a hidden lake of not-too-sweet chocolate sauce spiked with espresso. Make sure you have a bowl of cold, lightly whipped cream to serve with this, or a stash of vanilla ice cream.

150g unsalted butter, cut into pieces
330g self-raising flour
1½ tsp baking powder
180g light muscovado sugar
75g cocoa powder
250ml milk
4 large eggs
whipped cream or vanilla ice cream, to serve

For the topping:
85g light muscovado sugar
60g cocoa powder
50ml espresso coffee

Serves: 8 | Takes: 50 minutes

Place the butter in a 30 x 20 x 5-cm roasting tray. Preheat the oven to 160°C/325°F and while it reaches temperature place the tray inside for the butter to melt.

Meanwhile, whisk together the flour, baking powder, sugar and cocoa together in a mixing bowl.

When the butter has melted, pour into a jug and set aside to cool for a few minutes. Meanwhile, brush the tray with the residual butter so all the sides are coated.

Add the milk and eggs to the melted and cooled butter and mix well. Stir this into the dry ingredients to make a smooth batter. Scrape into the buttered roasting tray and smooth the top with a spatula.

Mix all the topping ingredients together with 450ml just-boiled water and pour over the batter. Bake for about 30 minutes until the top is firm: there will be a pool of sauce under the sponge. Serve hot topped with whipped cream or ice cream.

(Pictured overleaf)

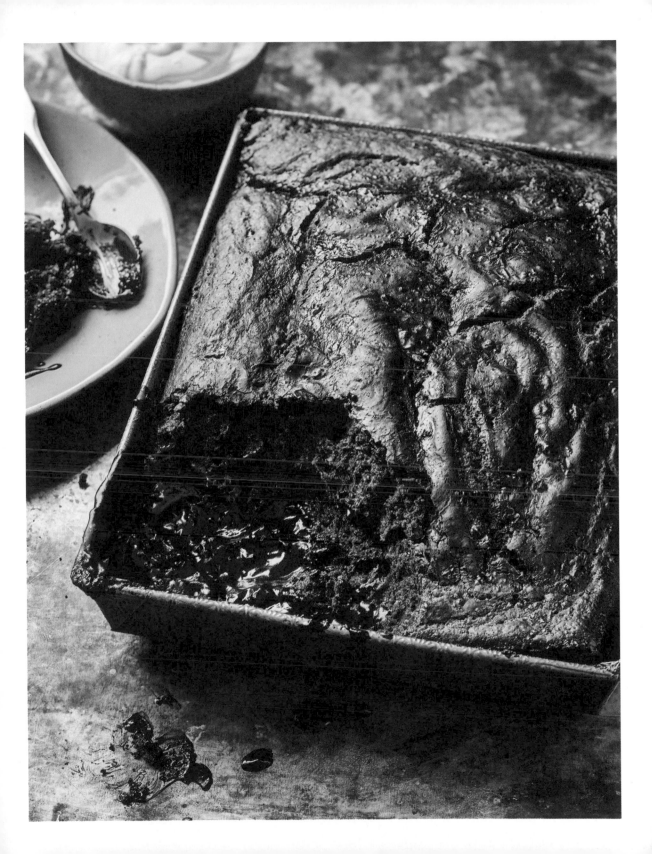

Roast pears in Marsala and saffron syrup

This simple but sumptuous pudding appeals to all the senses: it tastes and looks wonderful, and your kitchen will smell ambrosial while it's cooking. The grown-up flavours – booze, herbs and fruit – really sing together beautifully.

3 tbsp unsalted butter, cut into
   small pieces
100g light brown soft sugar
generous pinch of saffron
   strands, chopped
200ml sweet Marsala or medium sherry
2 tbsp lemon juice
1 rosemary sprig
4 firm but ripe pears, ideally Conference
   or William
200g mascarpone cheese
200g crème fraîche
2 tbsp icing sugar, sifted
1 vanilla pod, split in half lengthways
   and seeds scraped out
toasted flaked almonds, to serve
   (optional)

Serves: 4 | Takes: 1 hour

Preheat the oven to 200°C/400°F.

Place the butter, sugar and saffron in a 30 x 20 x 5-cm roasting tray and pour over 125ml just-boiled water. Stir to dissolve the sugar and melt the butter – it doesn't matter if there are still traces left. Stir in the Marsala and lemon juice, and add the rosemary sprig.

Peel and halve each pear, then scoop out the core with a teaspoon or melon baller. Transfer the fruit, cut-side down, to the roasting tray as you go, spooning over some of the liquid to stop it discolouring.

Roast for about 50 minutes, basting frequently, and gently turning the fruit over halfway through. When done, the pears should be very tender and the liquid reduced to lovely amber syrup.

Meanwhile, lightly whisk the mascarpone, crème fraîche, icing sugar and vanilla seeds together in a bowl. Chill in the fridge until needed.

Serve the pears with the syrup spooned over and topped with the mascarpone cream and flaked almonds, if you like.

Apple and almond tart with thyme

Fruity, buttery and fragrant with vanilla and thyme, this is a chic but very simple dessert inspired by the French classic *tarte fine aux pommes*. A scoop of vanilla ice cream or cloud of sweetened whipped cream (spiked with Calvados if you're feeling fancy) would be perfect on the side.

1 sheet of all-butter puff pastry, about 300g
50g ground almonds
30g caster sugar
1 vanilla pod, split in half lengthways and seeds scraped out
¼ tsp ground cinnamon
4 eating apples, about 400g
squeeze of lemon juice
2 tsp Demerara sugar
15g unsalted butter
few thyme sprigs

Serves: 4–6 | Takes: 40 minutes, plus 20 minutes chilling

Preheat the oven to 200°C/400°F and line a 30 x 20 x 5-cm roasting tray with baking parchment.

Trim the pastry into a 20 x 30 cm rectangle and transfer to the prepared tray. Mark out a 1-cm border with the back of a knife and prick the area inside the border all over with a fork.

Mix the almonds, caster sugar, vanilla seeds and cinnamon together in a small bowl. Break up any clumps of vanilla seeds by rubbing them between your fingers, as for butter into flour. Sprinkle evenly inside the pastry border. Chill in the fridge for at least 20 minutes.

Working quickly, peel, quarter and core the apples, then finely slice them, ideally on a mandoline. Transfer to a bowl as you go, tossing with a little lemon juice to prevent discolouration.

Tightly arrange overlapping apple slices in rows within the pastry border – if you're feeling artistic, place them all facing the same way, like fish scales. Sprinkle over the Demerara sugar, then dot with tiny pieces of the butter. Arrange the thyme sprigs on top and bake for 25 minutes, or until puffed and golden.

Coconut rice pudding with cardamom and kirsch cherries

Most countries have their own version of rice pudding, and this has a bit of a Scandinavian vibe, with the inclusion of cardamom, a favourite Nordic spice. It's a great dessert but also does nicely for breakfast if there's any left over.

30g unsalted butter, chopped into pieces, plus extra for greasing
400-ml can coconut milk
1.3l whole milk, or more if needed
200g pudding rice or other short-grain rice
50g golden caster sugar
3 cardamom pods, crushed with the side of a knife
3 short strips of lemon zest
pinch of sea salt
1 whole nutmeg, grated
1 can or jar of black cherries in kirsch syrup (any kind of non-boozy syrup is also fine)

Serves: 6 | Takes: 1 hour 40 minutes

Preheat the oven to 150°C/300°F and generously butter a 30 x 20 x 5-cm roasting tray or dish.

Pour both the milks into the prepared roasting tray and stir well, breaking up any thick blobs of coconut milk with the back of a spoon. Stir in all the remaining ingredients, except the cherries.

Bake for 1½ hours, stirring halfway through, until the rice is tender and creamy. Add a splash more milk if the rice threatens to dry out before it's cooked.

Remove the cardamom pods before serving with the black cherries and syrup spooned over.

index